THE SECRET ANCIENT CODE OF DANIEL

REVEALING THE LAST WEEK OF YEARS

2016 – The beginning of the last week of 7 years.

2016 – A year marked in time.

2016 – The year Mystery Babylon falls.

2016 – The most eventful year since the time Jesus Christ walked the earth.
What does this mean for America and the world?

BY HENRY A. RHYNE

First published May 2015

Published by Henry A. Rhyne

CHAPTER CONTENTS

1 - BOOK INTRODUCTION

The purpose of this book is to share information regarding the end times and the season we are in. It is important to know the season we are in, so that we can be prepared for the unfolding of prophetic events. We are not to fear or get distressed, but to rejoice, for the coming of our LORD is near.

The information presented here is what I call secret ancient knowledge. I believe this knowledge was in antiquity once widely known. But, over time it has largely been forgotten, over looked and lost.

Many people disregard this type of knowledge simply on the basis that it is old.

However, I believe this ancient knowledge and wisdom was originally handed down by God and given to man for a purpose – so that man would know God's seasons and times.

In it are the secrets of God and His timing of events. It is this secret ancient knowledge that Daniel knew. It is this secret ancient knowledge that unlocks what is hidden in Daniel and reveals the year that Mystery Babylon will fall, and it tells us of Daniel's last week of years – the end of days – the end of time.

The section on the year of the fall of Mystery Babylon, the year 2016 and all the great earth time numbers pointing to 2016 is the heart of this book.

When God gave me this, and I saw it unveiled I was stunned and amazed at how it all fits together. Hopefully you will find it quite remarkable as well.

I want to thank David Flynn for his book, "Temple At The Center Of Time", and Graham Hancock for his book, "Finger-Prints Of The Gods". These two books are what started the journey that led to this revelation concerning the fall of Mystery Babylon and all the information that points to the year 2016 as being unlike any other year.

David Flynn's book, "Temple At The Center Of Time", is where I first learned of the year ancient Babylon fell and that the writing on the wall added up to a very important number.

It was in Graham Hancock's book, "Finger-Prints Of The Gods", that I learned about what I call the great earth time numbers – about the movement of the equinox line through the constellations and the precession of the earth.

After reading their books, I studied Daniel again and started to meditate on all I had learned and then the LORD gave me new insight which is what I'm sharing with you.

The section on the year Mystery Babylon falls is what was written first. But, this of course raises certain related questions, and so I included other related topics as well. Some of these I had actually been looking into over the past year or two. God had revealed the other parts of this book first and then the part on year of the fall of Mystery Babylon. So, this book is written in the order I received it.

Finally, I have included a section that is a preview of two other books on the subject of animals and stewardship. My primary ministry is to build a bridge between Christians and animal lovers. The purpose is to help lead animal lovers to Christ and to help Christians understand their role as stewards of God's creatures and to generally teach what the Bible says about animals.

This preview section of two upcoming books is especially relevant in these last days.

Understanding the meaning of the word of God is of the utmost importance and none of us can afford to lack understanding of the word.

Simply knowing the word is insufficient. Satan knows the word, as do the fallen angels. The Pharisees likewise knew the word, but they lacked understanding, which is why they couldn't recognize Jesus as Christ and be saved. We are not instructed to read the word, but to study – so that we will not just know the word, but go to a higher level and gain an understanding of the word, so that we can truly be converted and saved. (Matt. 13:13-19)

Unfortunately, many who believe they are going to be with the LORD forever won't be – think of the story of the ten bridesmaids among others. We can't afford to lack understanding, because that allows us to be deceived.

I hope this book helps to increase your level of understanding and reveals to you the season we are now in.

May God Bless You, Always.

Henry Rhyne

2 - NEW YORK AND AMERICA

There is debate over what city is the biblical Mystery Babylon. And most people say that America is not in the bible. I believe America is in the Bible and it's not hard to find – and I also believe that the city of Mystery Babylon can be identified.

In biblical terms New York City is the city of Mystery Babylon and America is the wilderness and also is the eagle.

THE CITY REPRESENTS THE KINGDOM

The city of Mystery Babylon represents the Babylonian system which is a kingdom.

"And Cush begat Nimrod: he began to be a mighty one in the earth. He was a mighty hunter before (in defiance of) the LORD: wherefore it is said, Even as Nimrod the mighty hunter before (in defiance of) the LORD. And the beginning of his kingdom was Babel, and Erech, Accad, and Calneh in the land of Shinar." (Gen. 10:8-10 KJV) ('In defiance of' – added by author as it is the more accurate interpretation instead of 'before')

Here we see the beginning of the kingdom of Babylon – the beginning of the Babylonian system started by Nimrod who is a type of anti-Christ represented by the first man made city Babel or Babylon.

The city represents the system. The Babylonian system is in defiance of God. It is a man made system with an anti-Christ spirit, ultimately it is Satanic, because it is opposite of God's system (opposite as in opposed to). Within it is a governmental and economic system. There is also a culture of the times – today it is our pop-culture. And there is the same governmental and economic system we see ruling the earth today, controlled by the same anti-Christ spirit.

8

Part of the Babylonian system is the push into genetic modification. Today, not only are seeds and plants being genetically altered (including much farm produce), but animals are being genetically played with as well. This messing around with the genetic code of God's creation is very dangerous.

In Genesis chapter six we read about the fallen angels intermingling their DNA with man's and producing genetically altered beings – part human and part angelic – the nephilim. I believe these fallen angels were also tinkering around with animal DNA – corrupting their genetics as well. We see the images of half man – half animal, and animals with multi-species parts depicted in ancient art work in much of the world.

This corruption of God's creation, by playing with the genetics of His creation is one of the main reasons He brought the flood and destroyed the earth. The Bible says that in the last days it shall be as in the days of Noah.

Today scientists all over the globe are doing the very same thing the fallen angels did, which caused God to react by sending a flood and destroying all life – because it had been corrupted – the DNA was no longer what God had originally created.

In addition to this we have the push to integrate man and machine – to weave technology into the human body – creating borg (of Star Trek fame) like creatures. Again this is corrupting God's creation.

God does not change. This activity caused God to destroy everything in Noah's day and it will cause God to destroy everything today – as in the days of Noah.

Ultimately, this is man's attempt to become God like or to become a god. It is not only corrupting His creation – it is trying to become as a god – to get to heaven and achieve immortality in a way that is not according to God's way.

In Genesis chapter eleven we see the same thing with the building of the tower of Babel. Man trying to become a god – trying to get to eternal life, and achieve immortality outside of the way of God. And God destroys the tower because of it.

This is a main part of the reason God will likewise destroy the city of Mystery Babylon. God does not change.

God will not stand idly by while man wrecks His creation – He will destroy those who cause destruction here on earth. (See Revelation 11:18).

When we see the fall of the city of Mystery Babylon we will also be witnessing the fall of the entire Babylonian system – man's system, which is Satanic. This collapse of man's system will open the door for the return of the LORD and the setting up of His Kingdom here on earth.

But, before that happens Satan will have one last gasp which brings the anti-Christ and the tribulation period – Daniel's last week of years.

In Revelation we see the city of Mystery Babylon being destroyed quickly – in a single hour. Remember, the city represents the system.

That Great City Mystery Babylon

The Bible gives us vital clues as to the identity of that city and history gives us more clues - these together give us the identity very clearly.

Here is part of the description of Mystery Babylon from the KJV bible, in Revelation. (Bold and underline added)

"And there came one of the seven angels which had the seven vials, and talked with me, saying unto me, Come hither; I will show unto thee the judgment of **the great whore that sitteth upon many waters:** With whom the kings of the earth have committed fornication, and the inhabitants of the earth have been made drunk with the wine of her fornication.

So he carried me away in **spirit into the wilderness: and I saw a woman** sit upon a scarlet covered beast, full of names of blasphemy, having seven heads and ten horns. And the woman was arrayed in purple and scarlet color, and decked with gold and precious stones and pearls, having a golden cup in her hand full of abominations and filthiness of her fornication: And upon her forehead was a name written, MYSTERY BABYLON THE GREAT, THE MOTHER OF HARLOTS AND ABOMINATIONS OF THE EARTH." (Rev. 17:1-5 KJV bold and underline added)

Here the city of Mystery Babylon is represented as a woman.

She sits upon many waters (location). And this woman Mystery Babylon is located in the wilderness. So we have as the location a place in the wilderness that is surrounded by many waters.

The description these verses present is one of industry, trade and riches, one connected to all nations and whom influences all nations by her appetite and her riches and causes all nations to have relations with her – which speaks of trade and adopting her system. This system is the Babylonian system, man's system, an abomination to the LORD.

Revelation 17:18 KJV, "And the woman which thou sawest is that great city, which reigneth over the kings of the earth".

This city is a great city – big, highly influential. It reigns over the kings of the earth – all leaders and nations will try to appease her and do business with her so they can profit. This city is one where big businesses (Mega multinational corporations) headquarter and conduct business even to the point of influencing nations. In other words there is a mixing of these giant businesses and governments which is corrupt and corrupts much of the earth.

New York City is the preeminent city of commerce; The New York Stock Exchange (NYSE) and Nasdaq are the number one and two largest stock exchanges in the world. NYC is where leaders meet, where deals are done, it is one of the richest, if not the richest city in the world. The United Nations headquarters has been there since 1952.

There are three bull statues in place in the world (golden calves if you like). New York City has the first, which represents its financial significance and the worship of the financial system.

What other city has near as much of a world impact and influence as New York? There is no close second.

Read Revelation 18, it describes the city in more detail. It elaborates on the previous description, telling us how great, rich, powerful, and profitable the city is. There is none quite like this. It is also a port city where ships come and merchants trade. New York is a port city where ships come and merchants trade. NYC is the center of the economic system of the world today - and it sits upon many waters.

In fact before it was called New York – it was called New Amsterdam after Amsterdam in Europe. Amsterdam comes from Amstelredamme (dam in a watery area).

Amsterdam is a city that was built on the Amstel river, where a dam was constructed which created a port and harbor.

Amsterdam derived its name from being built on the Amstel river. Amsterdam is surrounded by water.

Here is what *www.amsterdam.info* says, "Amsterdam is the most watery city in the world. Its canals and harbors fill a full quarter of her surface. Its waterways have always been its essence and its source of wealth".

It has the oldest stock exchange (and a bull statue just like Wall Street); it was the center of commerce and trade in the 17th century.

So, Amsterdam could be one candidate for Mystery Babylon. But, Amsterdam is not as rich or influential today as New York.

New York was originally called New Amsterdam - loosely meaning New Land on many waters – very near the biblical phrase 'land upon many waters'.

While Amsterdam could possibly be the city, New York is a better fit.

New York has the top two stock exchanges today, the original bull statute and is a port city of enormous trade and commerce – the world center of economics, and the UN headquarters. New York has taken the place of Amsterdam and fits all the descriptions of Mystery Babylon.

Also, consider that at its foundation America was a vast wilderness.

While Native American Indians inhabited the area in fairly large numbers, they lived in a way that did not destroy or build up the land.

So, when first founded America was a wilderness. As we saw - the city of Mystery Babylon is located in the wilderness. (Revelation 17:3)

New York City is the City of Mystery Babylon.

3 - AMERICA IN THE BIBLE

America started as a wilderness. The national symbol of America is the eagle. And America was formed by rebelling and separating from England whose national symbol is a Lion.

Daniel has a vision he describes in chapter seven – here is verse 4 (KJV)

"The first was like a lion, and had eagle's wings: I beheld till the wings thereof were plucked, and it was lifted up from the earth, and made stand upon the feet as a man, and a man's heart was given to it."

Daniel is seeing the United States of America being born out of Great Britain.

In Ezekiel 17 we read about the eagle (America).

"1 And the word of the LORD came unto me saying,

2 Son of man, put forth a riddle, and speak a parable to the house of Israel; 3 And say, Thus saith the Lord GOD; A great eagle with great wings, long winged, full of feathers which had divers colors came unto Lebanon and took the highest branch of the cedar: 4 He cropped off the top of his young twigs, and carried it into a land of traffick; he set it in a city of merchants. 5 He also took the seed of the land, and planted it in a fruitful field; he placed it by great waters, and set it as a willow tree." (Ezek. 17:1-5 KJV)

This describes the Jews coming to America as a place of refuge. America has been the greatest haven of refuge for the Jewish people for about 350 to 360 years. The first Jews and most Jewish immigrants early on came to the port city of New York – a city of trade and merchants, and trafficking of goods.

The great eagle has great wings, long and full of feathers – indicating strength, a long reach of influence and full of blessings and prosperity. Diverse colors – a melting pot of peoples from many different nations.

The highest branch denotes a Christian nation, one that has accepted Jesus Christ as Lord – Jesus is the highest branch; and the land of traffick is New York, where historically most immigrants first arrived.

The land of traffick also represents Babylon (New York City aka New Amsterdam). The fruitful field represents the prosperity of America; the seed are the first Jews (and possibly also the first Christians – the Puritans) who came to America. Being placed by the great waters again identifies New York – a place near a lot of waterways and as a port where the immigrants arrived. The willow tree describes a healthy well watered, well nurtured, Godly, and blessed tree meaning people or nation.

These verses in Ezekiel are describing New York City and America as a place of refuge for the Jewish people.

Lets' go to Revelation and then we will come back to Ezekiel.

"1 And there appeared a great wonder in heaven; a woman clothed with the sun, and the moon under her feet, and upon her head a crown of twelve stars:

2 And she being with child cried, travailing in birth, and pained to be delivered.

3 And there appeared another wonder in heaven; and behold a great red dragon, having seven heads and ten horns, and seven crowns upon his heads.

4 And his tail drew the third part of the stars of heaven, and did cast them unto the earth: and the dragon stood before the woman which was ready to be delivered, for to devour her child as soon as it was born.

5 And she brought forth a man child, who was to rule all nations with a rod of iron: and her child was caught up unto God, and to his throne.

6 And the woman fled into the wilderness, where she hath a place prepared of God, that they should feed her there a thousand two hundred and threescore days." (Revelation 12:1-6 KJV)

I can't say I fully understand all of this. But, I do understand a good part.

HENRY A. RHYNE

There are multiple parallel lines of prophecy and revelation going on here.

Verses 1 and 2 Revelation 12 describes the birth of Jesus and the astronomical events during that time. The woman clothed in the sun is the constellation Virgo (the virgin) which was the constellation the sun rose in at autumn equinox at the time of the birth of Jesus Christ. The woman is also Mary, the virgin mother of Jesus, and by extension the nation of Israel and the Jewish people.

The dragon too is a lesser known constellation called Draco (located near the Little Dipper). This event in heaven is of course a stellar representation of the birth of Jesus; and Herod (Satan incarnate) trying to kill Him as soon as He is born by killing all the young Jewish males. (Verses 3 and 4 Revelation 12) And this is a parallel of Satan trying to kill the seed (the genetic line) that produces Jesus Christ.

Verse 5 Revelation 12 describes the King Jesus Christ and His later ascent to heaven after His death and resurrection.

In verse 6 Revelation 12, this is something that will occur in the future when the anti-Christ rules and tries to destroy the woman (who here is the nation of Israel). The thousand two hundred and threescore days is 1,260 days or a time, times and half a time. This can also be expressed as 3.5 years. (Note: 1,260 is half of 2,520 which is a 7 year shemitah period).

We also read of this in Daniel.

Revelation 17 verse 1, there is an angel telling John, that he will show him the judgment of the great whore that sits on many waters (location of Mystery Babylon is on many waters). In Revelation 17:3, John is taken in spirit into the wilderness where he sees the woman, (location is in the wilderness and on many waters). Revelation 17:5 we get the identification of this woman as the city of Mystery Babylon.

These verses above in Revelation go with Ezekiel 17.

In them we see common threads.

16

We see an eagle (which came from a lion), the wilderness, with the wilderness as a place of refuge for the Jewish people, and the city of (Mystery) Babylon located in the wilderness on many waters.

If we put this all together we can see America is the eagle and the wilderness, where the Jewish people take refuge, and also where the city of (Mystery) Babylon is located.

So, prophetically speaking we have identified the location of Mystery Babylon as New York City.

We have also identified America as the eagle and the wilderness. This is America in the Bible.

I believe there is a biblical prophecy that has just recently been fulfilled, at least as a parallel fulfillment. It involves America and it is concerning the verses that have to do with the woman (the Jewish people taking refuge in the wilderness for 3.5 years).

The woman represents the Jewish people (as well as the nation of Israel). The wilderness represents the United States of America. As a prophetic foreshadow of the actual prophetic event, the Jewish people will find refuge in America for 1,260 days or three and a half years.

This has been fulfilled – the Jewish people have found refuge in America for 350 plus years. (350 years is a multiple of times, time and half a time or of 1,260 days, 350*360= 126,000)

As a side note: Noah lived for 350 years after the flood, then a new age began. This (I believe) is the only place in the Bible where this exact length of time is mentioned.

The first officially recognized Jews came to America (a vast wilderness at the time and at its founding) in 1654. Solomon Pietersen came to New Amsterdam (New York City – Mystery Babylon) and a few days later twenty three other Jews came from Brazil, which at the time was called 'The Land of the Holy Cross'. The 23 had trouble being allowed in, and

Solomon Pietersen acting as their advocate secured their entry. These 24 can be looked at as the elders of Jews in America.

There were others who came from 'The Land of the Holy Cross', but who were not part of this group in any way. There may have also been other Jews who came prior to this – but these are largely recognized as the first official Jews in America.

To summarize 24 Jews (including Solomon Pietersen) (the elders) came to the great city of New Amsterdam in the vast wilderness of America from The Land of the Holy Cross. This little known piece of American history has biblical implications all over it.

America was a place of refuge and had the largest population of Jews anywhere on earth until very recently, officially beginning in 1654.

$1654 + 350 = 2004$.

Did anything significant happen in 2004? Yes.

From Wikipedia/Barack Hussein Obama 2nd as on 3/2/15 "In 2004, Obama received national attention during his campaign to represent Illinois in the United States Senate with his victory in the March Democratic Party primary, his keynote address at the Democratic National Convention in July, and his election to the Senate in November."

350 years from the time of first official Jews coming to New Amsterdam (Mystery Babylon) in the vast wilderness of America from 'The Land of The Holy Cross' for refuge, future president Barack Obama comes on the National scene in a big way. Barack Obama would become president of the United States in 2008; and he is arguably the most anti-Jewish, anti-Christian president in our nation's history.

Obama would go on to say, "America is no longer a Christian nation". The United States has under gone a dramatic shift since Barrack Obama has been elected – so his arrival on the political scene, his running for president and winning are all of great historic and prophetic significance.

America has changed. Obama came on the scene in 2004, exactly 350 years after 1654, and he represents the change of America. These events are markers in time, which have come about at their appointed time. And this marker in time denotes the end of one age and the beginning of another.

The prophetic foreshadow has to be complete before the actual prophetic fulfillment can occur – and the fore-shadow has just been completed.

Multiplication is a God principle. Satan is the opposite of God. Division is the opposite of multiplication. Wherever you see multiplication you are seeing the influences of God – where you see division you are seeing the influence of Satan.

Obama is arguably the most divisive president our nation has had in a great many years.

America is divided in many ways – by politics, by gender, by class, by race, and in other ways. This tells us who is having the greater influence.

There is more division coming – either in the form of states ceding from the union or from some sort of natural disaster that creates a physical division. The only thing that has kept us from the judgment of God at this point is our friendship with Israel as per Genesis 12:3. And now we are turning our back on Israel – this is very dangerous – the consequences will be severe.

350 years is a multiple of times, time and half a time, the length of time the Jews would find refuge in the wilderness.

350 years is the length of time Noah lived after flood – it is the only place in the Bible where this exact length of time is mentioned.

After those 350 years, Noah died, and a new age began here on earth.

After the three and half years of the tribulation a new era begins.

And we have the words of Jesus, "As it was in the days of Noah." (See Matt. 24:36-39)

I believe this 350 year period from the arrival of the first official Jews in America to Obama becoming a national figure are a parallel fulfillment of the prophecy we find in Revelation, signaling the start of a new age.

Keep in mind this group came to New Amsterdam (NYC aka Mystery Babylon) which is an area located on many waters in the vast wilderness of America from 'The Land of the Holy Cross' (Brazil) looking for a place of refuge, and the symbol of America is the eagle.

Compare this with the following verses, understanding the woman here represents the Jewish people.

"And the woman fled into the wilderness, where she hath a place prepared of God, that they should feed her there a thousand two hundred and threescore days". (Rev. 12:6 KJV)

"And to the woman were given two wings of a great eagle, that she might fly into the wilderness, into her place, where she is nourished for a time, and times, and half a time, from the face of the serpent". (Rev. 12:4 KJV)

This tells us the times we are in.

And this has identified the U.S. as the eagle and the wilderness. And it tells us that the United States of America was a place prepared by God, for the purpose of being a place of refuge for the Jews.

Israel and America are unique and have been from their very foundation. They are mirror images of each other, or opposite sides of the same coin.

At its foundation God chose the Jews and Israel as their land. At its foundation the first pilgrim settlers chose God, and America as their land.

One nation chosen by God at its founding, and another nation that chose God at its founding. In a way it is very similar to the book of Ruth.

Israel and America are the only two nations that so prominently have God at the very center of their founding – so they are connected and intertwined this way. So, we sometimes see biblical prophecies concerning Israel replaying or pre-playing in America. America has not replaced Israel, but is uniquely tied to Israel - like a mirror image.

I believe this mirror image of prophecy in Revelation has played out here in America. This was necessary before the actual prophecy could be fulfilled and it also means the actual fulfillment is at the door.

THE FUTURE OF AMERICA

Lets' go back to Ezekiel 17 starting from the beginning.

"1 And the word of the LORD came unto me saying,

2 Son of man, put forth a riddle, and speak a parable to the house of Israel; 3 And say, Thus saith the Lord GOD; A great eagle with great wings, long winged, full of feathers which had divers colors came unto Lebanon and took the highest branch of the cedar: 4 He cropped off the top of his young twigs, and carried it into a land of traffick; he set it in a city of merchants.

"5 He took also of the seed of the land, and planted it in a fruitful field; he placed it by great waters, and set it as a willow tree. 6 And it grew, and became a spreading vine of low stature, whose branches turned to him, and the roots thereof were under him: so it became a vine, and brought forth branches and shot forth sprigs.

7 There was also another great eagle with great wings and many feathers: and behold this vine did bend her roots toward him, and shot forth her branches toward him, that he might water it by the furrows of her plantation.

8 It was planted in a good soil by great waters, that it might bring forth branches, and that it might bear fruit, that it might be a goodly vine.

9 Say thou, Thus saith the Lord GOD; Shall it prosper? Shall he not pull up the roots thereof, and cut off the fruit thereof, that it wither? It shall wither in all the leaves of her spring, even without great power or many people to pluck it by the roots thereof. 10 Yea, behold, being planted, shall it prosper?

21

Shall it not utterly wither, when the east wind toucheth it? It shall wither in the furrows where it grew.

11 Moreover, the word of the LORD came unto me saying, 12 Say now to the rebellious house, Know ye not what these things mean? Tell them, Behold, the king of Babylon is come to Jerusalem, and hath taken the king thereof, and the princes thereof, and led them with him to Babylon; 13 And hath taken of the king's seed, and made a covenant with him, and hath taken an oath of him: he hath also taken the mighty of the land: 14 That the kingdom might be base, that it might not lift itself up, but that by keeping of his covenant it might stand.

15 But he rebelled against him in sending his ambassadors into Egypt, that they might give him horses and much people. Shall he prosper? Shall he escape that doeth such things? Or shall he break the covenant, and be delivered?

16 As I live, saith the Lord GOD, surely in the place where the king dwelleth that made him king, whose oath he despised, and whose covenant he brake, even with him in the midst of Babylon he shall die.

17 Neither shall Pharaoh with his mighty army and great company make for him in the war, by casting up mounts, and building forts, to cut off many persons: 18 Seeing he despised the oath by breaking the covenant, when, lo, he had given his hand, and hath done all these things, he shall not escape.

19 Therefore thus saith the Lord GOD; as I live, surely mine oath that he hath despised, and my covenant that he hath broken, even it will I recompense upon his own head.

20 And I will spread my net upon him, and he shall be taken in my snare, and I will bring him to Babylon, and will plead with him there for his trespass that he hath trespassed against me. 21 And all his fugitives with all his bands shall fall by the sword, and they that remain shall be scattered toward all winds: and ye shall know that I the LORD have spoken it.

22 Thus saith the Lord GOD; I will also take of the highest branch of the high cedar, and will set it; I will crop off from the top of his young twigs a tender one, and will plant it upon a high mountain and eminent:

23 In the mountain of the height of Israel I will plant it: and it shall bring forth boughs, and bear fruit, and be a goodly cedar: and under it shall dwell all fowl of every wing; in the shadow of the branches thereof shall they dwell.

24 And all the trees of the field shall know that I the LORD have brought down the high tree, have exalted the low tree, have dried up the green tree, and have made the dry tree to flourish: I the LORD have spoken and have done it." (Ezek. 17:1-24 KJV)

We can look at the beginning history of America in one particular way, from one particular perspective that is very general and very simplistic.

By looking at it in this way we can see this history as fulfilling Ezekiel 17. More correctly it fulfills part of Ezekiel 17 and part is yet to be fulfilled – so in Ezekiel 17 we have biblical prophecy telling us about the future of America.

At the founding of America there were two main groups of people (very generally speaking). There were the Puritans and other Christians as well as some Jews as one main group. This group believed in God and biblical principles; and the Puritans and other Christians came to America primarily to live out their faith, in a sense replaying the theme of Exodus, crossing the Atlantic as the ancient Jews had crossed the Red Sea. Along with them the Jews came for refuge to avoid persecution so they could practice their faith freely. Together this group is the good tree – the willow that becomes a good vine (Ezek. 17:5-6)

But, along with this first group came others who were not godly. They didn't care about God or the Bible or His principles for the most part.

This second group came to America for profit only. They saw the vast wilderness of America as a great supply of resources that could be exploited for profit. This group saw America and they saw dollar signs – that was their main focus. This is the second group mentioned in Ezekiel 17 (Ezek. 17:7-10)

Later in Ezekiel we read how these two trees (groups) grow up side by side – together in the same place. The second vine doesn't turn to God but tries to take advantage of the first vine. (Ezek. 17:7)

Eventually, we read in Ezekiel how God is going to uproot and tear out this second rebellious vine (Ezek. 17:9).

A mirror image of the covenant in Ezekiel 17 is America's covenant with God at its' founding and America's covenant with Israel and the Jewish people. Breaking this covenant is the mirror image of the breaking of the covenant in Ezekiel 17 and this is what triggers the fall of Mystery Babylon.

Further on, we read how this second vine has betrayed the LORD God by breaking its treaty, and ultimately God will bring down the high tree and exalt the low. The high tree is the second one, boastful, loud, with a lot of power and governmental influence – Babylonian in nature. The low tree is the first, truly Godly, of low stature, with less governmental influence and power, but following God and His principles.

The second tree that is uprooted which shall wither and die is Babylonian, and its' foundation is the city of Babylon – Mystery Babylon – New York City.

This is its foundation and from here it will be destroyed.

The uprooting of this tree is the destruction of Mystery Babylon – it is the same event we see in Revelation.

Note: (There is a precursor (and parallel) of the Jews coming out of Egypt and going into the wilderness of Sinai – and being carried on eagles wings in Exodus chapter 19)

Is America A Righteous Nation?

"A righteous man regardeth the life of his beast: but the tender mercies of the wicked are cruel." (Pr. 12:10 KJV)

The above verse is saying is that one of the evidences of a righteous man is that he treats his animals well. He is not made righteous by this – but it is an evidence of righteousness.

Likewise, commonsense would say that one treating their animals badly is evidence they are unrighteous.

God's principles are universal – they apply to people and nations alike – the only difference is the scale or level of degree.

We can apply this verse to a nation – a righteous nation regards the life of its animals.

Is America a righteous nation?

The evidence in this regard says no.

America allows all kinds of horrendous things to be done to its animals.

There are different figures depending on what source you use. But in America a dog or cat is euthanized every 10 to 16 seconds. That is about 5 per minute – 24 hours per day, 7 days per week or about Two million six hundred twenty eight thousand per year. (2,628,000 per year)

Our government rounds up wild horses, chasing them with helicopters and sends them to slaughter. Government agencies chase and kill wolves by helicopter and even gas wolf pups in their den.

And there are even group contests to see who can kill the most wolves – those who kill the most win prizes – as if killing is a good thing.

This is not a culture of God and life – it is a culture of death.

We have hundreds upon hundreds of animal testing facilities that perform all kinds of hellish experiments on animals and we have factory farms where some of the most horrible atrocities to animals take place – and many states will not allow what happens inside to be shown to the public.

They actually have laws against filming what is going on to hide it. They keep these things hidden from people – they keep these things in the dark and pass laws to prevent people from shining a light on the darkness.

Most people are unaware of what is really going on because it is hidden and it is hidden because they know if the public knew the truth they would be outraged. These animals can't speak up for themselves and need us to be their voice – we have a duty and obligation to God who placed us as stewards to stand up and shine a light on these horrific abuses.

America is a land of much sport hunting – killing God's animals for entertainment is widespread. Even canned hunting is now allowed in some places.

We allow things like bear baying, horse tripping and bull fighting.

We keep animals in a perpetual state of torture to manufacture pharmaceutics and health supplements.

Why not – they're just animals, right?

Wrong, they are God's creatures – they belong to him and we are supposed to be stewards – we have a duty and obligation to God to care for His animals.

America does not treat it animals well. This according to the Bible (the biblical principle) is evidence that America is not a righteous nation.

The Bible says that where immorality is widespread the government is easily toppled.

Immorality in a nation starts with how it treats its animals. What is acceptable in regards to treatment of animals will eventually become acceptable to do to people. If it is alright to harm and kill animals without just cause then it will become alright to do the same to people. After all, it is the same spirit, the spirit of causing pain, suffering and death – an anti Christ spirit.

First it is ok to harm and kill animals without just cause, and then it becomes ok to do that with people.

We all have the same creator.

All life comes from God, therefore all life is sacred.

Once that value disappears – it eventually disappears for all life.

When any life loses its value, all life loses its value.

When that happens it is the first stage of a cycle that leads to the collapse of a society – all societal values will likewise fall.

America has taken this path and now is far down the road. America has traded the culture of God and life for the culture of death.

Many people think if we fix two or three social issues everything will great again – it will mean we have turned back to God. No. That is just the surface level – it does not address the deeper issue, which is us truly turning to God in our hearts on all levels in all ways.

The only thing that is saving us from the judgment of God right now is our relationship with Israel and that is changing. If and when we turn on Israel (break our covenant as we saw in Ezekiel), judgment will come harshly and swiftly. And it is happening right now.

The falling of the city of Mystery Babylon will be part of that judgment.

AMERICA AFTER THE FALL OF MYSTERY BABYLON

What happens to America after the fall of Mystery Babylon?

America starts as a great wilderness. Biblically, the wilderness ultimately remains a wilderness. The wilderness itself does not change. It starts as a wilderness and ends up as a wilderness. This is the pattern where the wilderness is a place of testing and of finding God.

There is an exception where God causes the wilderness to flourish and become fruitful such as with the nation of Israel. Israel was at a time mostly desert but it has become very fruitful. We also see this with America, but it has changed.

In Revelation we are told that once Mystery Babylon falls it won't ever be inhabited again except by wild animals (Rev.17:19-24, Rev. 18:1-3).

This description resembles the effects of a nuclear explosion.

In Chernobyl, Russia, after their nuclear plant had a meltdown the whole area became off limits to people and is still abandoned to this day. It is too radioactive for humans and has become a wilderness. The whole area now is seeing the return of forests and wild forest animals. The animal's life spans are short because of the radiation, but they are otherwise flourishing in this newly created wilderness zone.

This is similar to the after effects we read about concerning Mystery Babylon. Mystery Babylon (New York City) will likely fall due to a major nuclear event.

When this happens, the rest of America and even the world will be impacted. The Babylonian system will start to collapse and with it much of America's prosperity. America will come to resemble America at its beginning. America will not be destroyed, but have areas of population with local economies and prosperity – and there will be other areas largely unpopulated and left alone – wilderness areas.

Ultimately, after Mystery Babylon falls, the low vine, the ones who believe in God and follow Him will be protected and caused to prosper. These groups in different areas will fare far better than the rest – although things will be very different than from today. Many things that we think of as important today will not be. Things will be greatly changed.

The wilderness speaks of a place where people are tested, and endure trials, but at the same time are protected and provided for (blessed); and in the process people find God and become much closer to Him, or if they deny God they die in the wilderness. The wilderness (and 40) is a place of transition.

This is the destiny of America.

If we want to know the end then we should look at the beginning, for the end is similar to the beginning. We see this in the Bible. In the bible when God's Kingdom is set up here on earth as described in Revelation 21 and 22; we see similar attributes to the Garden of Eden in the very beginning.

We can view the entirety of the bible and all of history as being about one singular thing. It is all about God fulfilling His original will and intention which was demonstrated in the Garden of Eden. God never changes – His will and intention then, is still and always His will and intention – it has not changed.

In the beginning, in the Garden of Eden was man and animals living together, in harmony in the presence of the LORD God, in paradise for all eternity (there was no death). This is still His ultimate will – it hasn't changed.

The entire course of history, the entirety of the Bible, the coming of Jesus Christ as a man, dying on the cross, being resurrected, the rise and fall of nations – all of it is about one thing – God's original plan and purpose. It is all about Him fulfilling His original will and intention. The end will resemble the beginning.

As for America, after the fall of Mystery Babylon and prior to the return of our LORD, it likewise will resemble what it did at the beginning.

At the beginning America was a vast wilderness with many pockets of civilization and populations of Native Americans. It was decentralized. This is similar to how it will be again. It will be decentralized, with many pockets of civilization and population centers in a great wilderness. There will still be a union but it won't be as strong as it is today.

Once Mystery Babylon falls and the Babylonian system starts to collapse people will leave America in droves, the population will decrease. It will all be too much for our government to handle. While the government will still exist – it will be more like the beginning, with limited reach, power and influence. We will see a decentralizing of power and the forming of smaller communities of people where the local governmental authorities have greater power and influence. America will be more like it was in the beginning, at its early founding.

Mystery Babylon represents the system and the system is spiritual, governmental, economic and cultural.

The Babylonian system – man's system - is ultimately a satanic system because it is opposite God's system.

We are told to come out of Babylon – this means for God's people to come out of the system as well as the city. We are to be in God's system, not Babylon's.

MY TWO DREAMS ABOUT AMERICA AND NEW YORK CITY

One night as I was working on other books I had this dream: I was with a small group of people in a large field. A short distance away was a train flying down the tracks very fast. Those of us in the field could see the tracks up ahead ended at a high cliff. Looking down from the edge of cliff - the bottom was beyond sight, but there was a bottom very far down. We saw the train barreling ahead toward the cliff unaware of what was ahead. We could see the people inside milling about in normal activities – some were eating, some reading the newspaper, others sitting at a bar drinking, and a woman dressed in red with a drink in her hand was slowly swaying to the music, and there was a little boy with his face pressed against the window looking at us curiously.

Our small group in the field saw the danger; we knew the train was rapidly heading for the cliff. We were jumping up and down, yelling and screaming trying to get their attention to warn them, but they didn't see or hear us, except the little boy who didn't understand. The train kept speeding toward the cliff and then the first cars went over, and then more and more cars went over the edge.

All of a sudden the people inside the train realized what was happening, and they tried to stop, but it was too late. The weight and momentum of the cars that had gone over the edge were pulling the whole train over. Inside people started to panic and scream, but there was nothing they could do and nothing we could do. All we could do at this point was watch as the entire train went over the cliff, disappearing and crashing below.

We just turned and walked away.

I believe the train is America – the people on the train are most of the people in America. (possibly all unsaved people everywhere) The small group in the field are the true believers and watchers sending out the warning.

A second dream: A while back I had a dream of what I believe was New York City – The Fall of Mystery Babylon.

I was on a bridge facing the city and I saw the other bridges on either side start to fall into the water, like they broke in half and collapsed, cars tumbling into the waterway.

Then I am given an aerial view as the bridge I was on collapses. Looking out I see the entire city – everywhere buildings are falling, all of them. There are hundreds, maybe thousands of fires, and water is flooding the streets – it is a strange combination. There is lots of destruction – the whole city is destroyed and burning as far as the eye can see. It is a catastrophic scene of devastation with nothing left standing. The entire landscape is turned into a vast smoldering wasteland.

I was never given any identifying land marks other than a group of bridges near each other and lots of buildings of all sizes. I believe it was New York City and what I was seeing was the fall of Mystery Babylon.

31

4 - THE YEAR MYSTERY BABYLON FALLS

Setting Dates?

Some people may say that the section on the year of the fall of Mystery Babylon is setting dates and that we are not supposed to set dates.

This is not setting dates exactly. This study and revelation is signaling the times and season we are in. In this discussion I never claim to know the day or hour of the return of Jesus Christ or of the rapture.

However, I do believe it is possible to know the season, the year, and possibly the month of the fall of Mystery Babylon and the year and season of the return of our Lord and of the rapture.

"But of the times and the seasons, brethren, ye have no need that I write unto you. For yourselves know perfectly that the day of the Lord so cometh as a thief in the night. For when they shall say, Peace and safety; then sudden destruction cometh upon them, as travail (pains) upon a woman with child; and they shall not escape. **But ye, brethren are not in darkness, that that day should overtake you as a thief.**" (1st Thess. 5:1-4 KJV)(Bold added)

Here, we are told that we are not in darkness, so that day won't overtake us a thief. It will only come on those who are sleeping, who are unaware, suddenly as a thief in the night. So, we as believers who are awake and studying and paying attention will know the times.

"Remember therefore how thou hast received and heard, and hold fast, and repent. If therefore thou shalt not watch, I will come on thee as a thief, and thou shalt not know what hour I will come upon thee." (Rev. 3:3 KJV)

Again, here Jesus is coming on those who are not watching as a thief.

So, logic tells us that if we are watching he won't come on us as a thief.

Further, I believe that Jesus Christ not only wants us to know this but expects us to know this and is displeased if we don't.

Most people who say we shouldn't set dates get that idea from Matthew 24:36. I don't think that is what the LORD is saying.

Matthew 24 begins with His disciples asking Him when the end times will be.

"And as he sat upon the Mount of Olives, the disciples came unto him privately, saying, Tell us when shall these things be? And what shall be the sign of thy coming, and of the end of the world?" (Matt. 24:3 KJV)

Note that 'end of the world' actually means end of the age.

Jesus answers by giving a whole list of signs to look for. This brings up the question – why would Jesus tell us what to look for if we are not supposed to know the season? Obviously, He wants us to know the season.

After going through many of the signs, Jesus says in verse 36, "But of that day and hour knoweth no man, no, not the angels of heaven, but my Father only."

Here the Lord is simply telling us that no man can accurately calculate or figure out the day or hour of His return and the rapture. It is impossible to know the exact moment.

Jesus is only referring to His return here and the rapture – nothing else.

Neither is He telling us that we shouldn't know the season, the year or even the month. In fact, I believe He absolutely wants us to at least know the season and maybe even the year and the month.

In Matthew 24:32-33 (KJV), we read "Now learn a parable of the fig tree; When his branch is yet tender, and putteth forth leaves, ye know summer is nigh: So likewise ye, when ye shall see all these things, know that it is near, even at the doors".

Again, obviously, our Lord wants us to know the season. Also, notice that He says, LEARN the parable. He doesn't say, here is the parable or this is the parable. He says LEARN the parable. What does that mean?

It means we are to study it and figure it out.

This fits in with 2nd Timothy 2:15 (KJV), "Study to show thyself approved unto God, a workman that needeth not to be ashamed, rightly dividing the word of truth."

Also, note that Jesus berates the Pharisees and Saducees for not knowing the season during His time. (Matt 16:1-3 KJV) "The Pharisees also with the Saducees came, and tempting desired him that he would show them a sign from heaven. He answered, and said unto them, 'When it is evening ye say, It will be fair weather: for the sky is red. And in the morning, It will be foul weather today, for the sky is red and lowering. O ye hypocrites, ye can discern the face of the sky; but can ye not discern the signs of the times?'".

So, here we see Jesus Christ calling them hypocrites for not recognizing what season it is. And, I believe this is a reference to the star of Bethlehem signaling His birth and thus the times. If they had recognized the star of Bethlehem (the astronomical events) they would have known it was the season for the arrival of the Messiah. But, they didn't – and so Jesus Christ calls them hypocrites.

Also, note Luke 19:41-44 (KJV)

"41 And when he was come near, he beheld the city, and wept over it, 42 Saying, 'If thou hadst known, even thou, at least in this thy day, the things which belong unto thy peace! But now they are hid from thine eyes.

43 For the days shall come upon thee, that thine enemies shall cast a trench about thee, and compass thee round, and keep thee in on every side,

44 And shall lay thee even with the ground, and thy children within thee, and they shall not leave in thee one stone upon another; because thou knewest not the time of thy visitation.'"

Here Jesus is prophesying about the destruction of Jerusalem – which later happened in 70 AD. And He gives the reason Jerusalem will be destroyed – because thou knewest not the time of thy visitation. According to these verses the reason Jerusalem is destroyed is because the people there didn't know the times – they didn't know the days of the LORD's coming.

Lastly, on this topic let's look at (Matthew 13:14-15 KJV), "And in them is fulfilled the prophecy of E-sa-ias, which saith, BY HEARING YE SHALL HEAR, AND SHALL NOT UNDERSTAND; AND SEEING YE SHALL SEE, AND SHALL NOT PERCIEVE: FOR THIS PEOPLE'S HEART IS WAXED GROSS AND THEIR EARS ARE DULL OF HEARING, AND THEIR EYES THEY HAVE CLOSED; LEST AT ANY TIME THEY SHOULD SEE WITH THEIR EYES AND HEAR WITH THEIR EARS, AND SHOULD UNDERSTAND WITH THEIR HEART, AND SHOULD BE CONVERTED, AND I SHOULD HEAL THEM."

What Jesus is saying is that these people are spiritually blind and deaf. They can't be healed (greek- iaomai – freed, made whole), because they lack understanding.

This is the condition of the church today and many people who call themselves Christians. They don't have understanding; they are spiritually blind and not really saved, not made whole and can't or won't even try to study and discern the times.

Understand, the people Jesus is referring to here are the Pharisees. These people know the scriptures, they attend and lead the church (the temple), they tithe, they observe all sorts of religious ceremonies, yet they aren't saved. They can't be converted because they lack understanding.

See, it is one thing to know the word and quite another to understand the meaning. Just knowing the word is not enough, understanding the meaning is vital.

According to the word of God we are to study, learn and understand. If we turn a deaf ear or blind eye to the Lord we are in disobedience.

This is what many Christians do. Many Christians and even Christian leaders today have religion but not relationship with the Lord. They know the word, they attend and lead church, are careful to say grace before every meal, but it is not real. They have religion- but not a true personal relationship with Jesus, therefore, though they know the word, they lack understanding, and because they lack understanding they are not truly converted, not made whole, and not truly saved. They are modern day Pharisees.

This unfortunately is a lot of the church today – better but not whole, knowing the word, but not understanding, and not able to discern the times or just not interested.

As the LORD Jesus says, let no man deceive you.

Always check what you hear and see with the word and the Holy Spirit –discern the spirit of truth.

That includes what is in this book

I believe you brethren are different – if you are reading this then you are studying to show yourself approved and trying to discern the times as we should, increasing in the spirit of Christ and gaining understanding – being converted and made whole through our LORD and SAVIOR Jesus Christ.

And so we continue in the spirit of Christ; and understand the times and seasons, so that great day of the Lord does not come upon us as a thief in the night. But rather we are studying, watching, and we are aware.

That is what we are supposed to do according to the word of God, and what we are doing. Not setting dates exactly, but knowing and understanding the season.

"It is the glory of God to conceal a thing: but the honor of kings is to search out a matter". (Proverbs 25:2 KJV)

Halleluiah!

THE SEED IS PLANTED

This topic came to me unexpectedly. I believe God led me to this and guided me throughout unraveling this secret.

One day I randomly picked up two books out of my library and started skimming through them. I'm not even sure where they came from or how I got these books. But something that day drew me to them.

These two books are "Finger-Prints of the Gods", by Graham Hancock, and "Temple at the Center of Time", by David Flynn.

As I skimmed through these I was immediately fascinated by the section concerning Ancient Babylon in David Flynn's book and by the sections in Graham Hancock's book having to do with what I call 'God's Great Earth Time Clock' – this has to do with the constellations and the basic astronomy regarding the large cycles of the earth and time.

A few days after I had read through these sections I had a thought, which I had many years before. It is a rather obvious one – that Ancient Babylon and Mystery Babylon are deeply connected.

We know that they are connected because John (in Revelation) calls the future great city that will be destroyed Mystery Babylon. Since he uses the term 'Babylon' he is obviously linking the two together.

I believe John saw into the future (our current times) and saw a city that in many ways resembled Ancient Babylon – it had the same spirit, the same economic system and same culture – thus 'Babylon'. This is the part John recognized. But, John didn't recognize the landscape – the geography, this part was a mystery to him. So he calls this great city which will fall, "Mystery Babylon".

LINKED IN TIME

I submit that Ancient Babylon and Mystery Babylon are not only linked by spirit, culture, governmental and economic system, but that they are also linked in time.

I believe they are linked in such a way as to be significant markers of time – imagine a chain representing the length of time between the two events – the fall of Ancient Babylon and the fall of Mystery Babylon.

This chain length of time is attached to Ancient Babylon in the past and to Mystery Babylon in the future. They are eternally linked and fixed in time, set and appointed – and not variable, they are connected by spirit, and by time. The fall of both are two set anchor points in time – linked and connected by a predetermined fixed length of time. This fixed length of time is set and can't be altered.

We know this Babylonian system begins with Nimrod in Genesis 10:8-10. This was the beginning of his kingdom, which is a system.

The city of Mystery Babylon is the embodiment of that system and when that great city falls, so will the whole Babylonian system. The world will be dramatically changed, and we will know for sure that we are in the last of the last days.

When we see this event happen we will know that we are in the closing days of the end of the age – the end of time.

DANIEL – MAN OF GOD, PROPHET, MATHEMATICIAN, ASTRONOMER

I had a second thought concerning all this. I believe that we are looking at Daniel's account of the fall of Ancient Babylon incorrectly or incompletely. We have been looking at it as only a historical account.

Why?

Who was Daniel?

Daniel was a prophet of God.

He was a prophet!

What if his account of the fall of Ancient Babylon is not only historic, but is also prophetic concerning the fall of Mystery Babylon?

In Revelation John connected the two.

Daniel was a prophet of the living God, so why shouldn't we look at the account of the fall of Ancient Babylon as prophetic as well as historic?

What if hidden within the account somewhere is a great secret that foretells when Mystery Babylon will fall? Could Daniel have given us secret hidden information that reveals when Mystery Babylon will fall?

I believe the answer is yes.

The account of the fall of Ancient Babylon is in fact prophetic and hidden within it is the secret of when Mystery Babylon will fall.

Another long held belief came back to me – it first came to light from watching Rick Larson's DVD, 'The Star of Bethlehem', Daniel was a master at astronomy. Daniel had been taken to Babylon which is east of Jerusalem. He never returns – he stays in Babylon. And in the account of the birth of Jesus Christ we see the wise men coming from the east to worship the new born king, because they saw His star (the star of Bethlehem).

The wise men came from the area where Daniel had been hundreds of years earlier. Daniel was important in Babylon and likely had students and followers whom he taught and instructed. They would have likely passed on Daniel's teachings through generations.

Those looking for a star signaling the birth of a Jewish king were likely of Jewish descent. To recognize this astronomical event would have taken serious astronomical knowledge.

I believe this knowledge was ultimately passed down from Daniel.

With all this I went back and read Daniel again. This time I saw many things I had never seen before – I believe the Holy Father opened my eyes and showed me these things.

I realized that Daniel was a great mathematician.

In Daniel we see precise numbers regarding the prophetic end time events. Why is it Daniel that receives these precise numerical time frames? Because, Daniel understood math, and astronomy and what I call 'The great earth time clock' created by God.

There are math terms sprinkled through the book of Daniel, some obvious - many hidden. We also see that Daniel and his three friends (Hananiah, Mishael and Azariah) were very wise and gifted, that God had blessed them with special knowledge and understanding.

Daniel 1:3-4 (KJV) "And the king spake unto Ashpenaz the master of his eunuchs, that he should bring certain of the children of Israel, and of the king's seed, and of the princes; Children in whom was no blemish, but well favoured, and skilful in all wisdom, and cunning in knowledge, and understanding science, and such as had ability in them to stand in the king's palace, and whom they might teach the learning and the tongue of the Chaldeans."

Daniel 1:17 "As for these four children, God gave them knowledge and skill in all learning and wisdom: and Daniel had understanding in all visions and dreams". (KJV)

Daniel 1:19-20 (KJV) "And the king communed with them; and among them all was found none like Daniel, Hananiah, Mishael, and Azariah: therefore stood they before the king. And in all matters of wisdom and understanding, that the king enquired of them, he found them ten times better than all the magicians and astrologers that were in his realm".

In Daniel 7:1 we read, "In the first year of Belshazar king of Babylon Daniel had a dream and visions of his head upon his bed: then he wrote the dream and told the sum of the matters". (KJV)

The sum of the matters! Who speaks like this? This is how a mathematician would speak.

In Daniel there is an undercurrent of math language and we are told in a number of places that Daniel was given special knowledge and understanding by God.

Daniel along with being very spiritual, and a prophetic man of God, was also a great astronomer and mathematician.

We need to understand who Daniel was, and the fact that he was also a mathematician and astronomer, as well as a prophet, in order to know how to unlock the secret of Daniel's historic account of the fall of Ancient Babylon – and to decipher its hidden prophetic meaning.

The sum of these thoughts is: Ancient Babylon is deeply connected to Mystery Babylon; Daniel is a prophet and also an astronomer and mathematician, and the account of the fall of Ancient Babylon somehow tells us the time of the future fall of Mystery Babylon.

We can uncover this if we look into what Daniel said in light of some basic astronomy and math; for these are the keys that will unlock the secret of when Mystery Babylon will fall.

The sum of these thoughts caused me to start investigating.

That was the thought process that brought me to the beginning of this study. God guided me through this – for I had no ability or knowledge of these things on my own – but was led to this amazing discovery.

This discovery reveals when that great city Mystery Babylon will fall.

Before we proceed, I want to thank Father God for revealing this to me.

Also, I want to thank Graham Hancock and David Flynn for their books, 'Finger-Prints of the Gods' and 'Temple at the Center of Time', respectively. The information in their books provided the initial steps in this journey.

MYSTERY BABYLON WILL FALL

BACKGROUND INFORMATION

This is truly exciting. This is a mystery of epic proportions and we will solve it. And by solving this mystery we will discover a great deal more about God's great - magnificent plan, and where we are in the end times.

Before we get to that, we need to discuss what Mystery Babylon is and what it represents. Then we need to look at Ancient Babylon and the book of Daniel for clues to find the secret code that reveals the year – to do this we need to examine some basic numbers and unlock their hidden secrets.

We see the Babylonian system all around us today. For example, the amount of time that the average person spends engaged in some type of media viewing has increased dramatically. At the same time the proportion of advertising within all media is increasing. More and more time and more and more dollars are being spent on advertising. People are being bombarded with advertising all the time. All of this advertising drives consumerism and materialism. So, we have this Babylonian triangle of advertising – consumerism – materialism that is everywhere.

People are being brainwashed to place huge importance on things. There is a constant pursuit of more and more things. People believe that if they have the latest and greatest product, their life will be complete and they'll be happy and fulfilled.

It's all a huge deception. It is Babylonian at its core, and it leads many astray. It even leads many who call themselves Christians into a shallow and superficial version of Christianity – a non spiritual version of Christianity, where there is no real relationship with Christ.

This group of people is deceived, they think they're saved, but really aren't. They worship things rather than the LORD – they are lukewarm, because they have been seduced by the Babylonian system. It is very dangerous and is all around us – even in the church. The bible tells us to come out of Babylon. This doesn't just mean the city – it means come out of the Babylonian system. Put the LORD first.

Similarly, we see a worship of the almighty dollar. This has gotten to a point where the only value anything has is the profit it can generate. Does a piece of land have value? Only if the lumber can be sold or only if the land can be developed. This is the mentality that rules today. Nothing has intrinsic value. The fact that God created it, that God's creatures live there means nothing – it is all about the dollars.

The point is the Babylonian system has taken over almost everywhere.

It is a system about values, about principles, about function and process, it is God's system vs. man's system. It is the almighty dollar vs. almighty God, spirituality vs. carnality.

Which are you going to follow? What happens when what you value is gone? What if the dollar collapses? What if your things are destroyed? What do you have then? What's really important?

The Babylonian system is a system controlled by short term, finite thinking. It denies eternity. God's system is infinite and eternal. We are called to think higher, bigger, long term and from everlasting to everlasting. We should expand our minds and grow from natural and material to spiritual – this is preparation time for eternity. It is time to grow from religion to relationship.

We also see the huge influence of pop culture – the worship of celebrities, and politicians and other pop culture personalities. But, what is their belief, and what is the foundation of that belief? People are following other people who are spiritually dead. This is the blind leading the blind. This has infected the church too. How many so called Christians fawn over celebrities or put them on a pedestal?

We even see some politicians and pop culture icons claiming to be Christians and their fruit is the exact opposite. And most of the church runs to them simply because they claim to be Christian. The vast majority of these people are not true Christians. They are leading people into deception just as Christ said.

"4 And Jesus answered and said unto them, 'Take heed that no man deceive you.

5 For many shall come in my name, saying, I am Christ; and shall deceive many'". (Matt. 24:5-6 KJV)

This is saying that many will come (not a few, but many), saying that Jesus is the Christ – and many will be deceived, and will follow deceivers just because they say Jesus is the Christ.

This is what we see in politics and pop culture and even in the church, with some ministries. Just because someone claims that Jesus is the Lord, that doesn't make them a true Christian – beware! Don't be deceived. This too is part of the Babylonian system – because ultimately it is a system of deception, of Satan, not of God.

The headquarters of this system is the city of Mystery Babylon – this is where the corruptive influence stems from – where the roots of it are.

America is no longer the land of the free – it is the land of big business and special interests, and political correctness and favoritism. This is a corrupted system, a Babylonian system. And America has been, and is, exporting this system worldwide. The exportation of this system is perhaps our largest export. New York City is the city where this system's roots are.

The city of Mystery Babylon will fall soon.

And, when we see the destruction of the city Mystery Babylon we will also see the destruction of the entire Babylonian system – the city represents the kingdom (or system).

This will be the end of man's rule – ultimately opening the door to bring about the rule and kingdom of Jesus Christ our Lord and Savior.

ANCIENT BABYLON

Ancient Babylon was destroyed in 539 BC. It was right after Daniel read the writing on the wall.

In Daniel chapter five we read that King Belshazzer has a big party and drinks from the sacred gold cups that had been taken from the temple in Jerusalem by his predecessor – King Nebuchadnezzar.

Then a mysterious hand writes something on the wall that terrifies the king and he ends up bringing in Daniel to read and interpret the writing and Daniel does so.

"This is the message that was written: MENE, MENE, TEKEL, PARSIN. This is what these words mean:

MENE, MENE - means 'numbered' – God has numbered the days of your reign and has brought it to an end.

TEKEL - means 'weighed'- you have been weighed on the balances and have failed the test.

PARSIN - means 'divided' – your kingdom has been divided and given to the Medes and Persians." (Daniel 5:25-28,Tyndale NLT)

(Note the numerical terms – numbered, weighed, divided.)

That very night the king was killed and his kingdom given to Darius the Mede.

This happened on October 12th, 539 BC., which on the biblical calendar would have been Tishri 16 that year. (Tishri 1 is Rosh Hashana – the Jewish New Year)

MENE, TEKEL and PARSIN are monetary terms (and the sum is also a length of time).

MENE is 1,000 gerahs,

TEKEL is 20 gerahs,

PARSIN is 500 gerahs.

A gerah is just a unit of currency – like the dollar.

So, MENE, MENE, TEKEL, PARSIN adds up to 2,520.

(1,000+1,000+20+500=2,520)

We can also get 2,520 like this. 7*360=2,520.

2,520 (days) is also a 7 year shemitah period. (7*360=2,520)

As a side note: half of 2,520 is 1,260 (as in Daniel's later prophecy)

Daniel sees the writing on the wall – 'Mene, Mene, Tekel, Parsin' – He immediately recognizes the numeric value of 2,520 (a shemitah period) and he interprets this to mean Ancient Babylon's days had been numbered, the king weighed and found lacking and that the kingdom would be divided – all from these words and the numeric values.

SECRETS HIDDEN IN NUMBERS

THE SECRET ANCIENT KNOWLEDGE OF DANIEL

Numbers are a universal language of the LORD like the stars (astronomy) and nature (seasons, seeds and fruit). As you read through these sections don't just look at the numbers and math, but try to understand the meaning – what the numbers are saying – ultimately this is the most important aspect of what follows.

At this point we need to look at some important numbers and understand their significance and how they all fit together to really comprehend the mystery and plan concerning the fall of Mystery Babylon.

The numbers are the foundation which will join it all together.

Every number we find in relation to the year of the Fall of Mystery Babylon has to be significant – if any number lacks significance then we don't have it – if it is of God all the numbers have to be significant.

Here is the background on some important numbers we need to examine.

1 – The beginning, Day 1 is the first day – the beginning

2 – The first number of multiplication (and also division) one times any number or any number divided by one equals the original number. Two is the first whole number which can multiply or divide. The widow woman in the story with Elijah gathers 2 sticks – after that we see multiplication of her meal and oil. (see 1 Kg. chapter 17)

3 – The number of divinity. Father, Son and Holy Ghost. Number of Jesus Christ – the number three is all over the birth, life, death and resurrection of Jesus.

4 – The biblical number of the earth (4 pts on a compass, 4 corners etc. 4 seasons)

5 – The number of grace, David picks up 5 stones and uses these to defeat the enemy- Goliath.

6 - The number of man (man and land animals created on the sixth day) Noah was 600 years old when the flood came.

7 – The number of completion, (7 days of creation, 7 days per week, 7 years in a shemitah, 7 seals, etc) means completion, totality, perfection.

8 – The number of new beginnings (1st day of new week, 8 people in Noah's ark)

9- The number of finality – it is the last single number, Jesus went on the cross at the 3rd hour, and at the ninth hour He gave up the ghost and cried out, "It is Finished", 9=finality, 9th hour is the final hour.

10- The number of heaven – or God's Kingdom. Why is the number 40 so important? It is the earth number 4 multiplied by the heaven number 10 – multiplying earth by heaven. In Luke 19 Jesus tells a parable of the Kingdom of Heaven in which 10 servants are given 10 pounds. 10 = heaven, the tithe is a tenth, the 10 commandments

12 – The number of divine government, divine rule (12 tribes, 12 disciples, 12 months, 12 main constellations)

40 – A period of testing and trials, of coming closer to God. A time where one is set aside for God, protected by Him, and provided for. One enters carnal and of the earth and emerges spiritual, Godly. (4*10)

72 – An earth time number – the number of years it takes for the spring or fall equinox line to move 1 degree. Also (12*6) (divine rule times man); I believe this is a biblical generation.

360- A Number of earth time, (360 degrees of the earth, 360 days in a biblical year – also represents a full cycle of time) (5*72)

365- A number of earth time, (365 days in a solar year, Enoch was taken in his 365th year)

2,160 - Approximate diameter of the moon 2,160 miles, and most important - it is the number of years it takes the equinox line to move through each constellation - part of the great earth time clock. **(6*360=2,160)** number of man times biblical year. Noah was 600 years old when the flood came – 600*360 =216,000.

2,520 - Mene, Mene, Tekel, Parsin, Also, 2,520/7=360 or **7*360=2,520**, the number of days in a shemitah period, an earth time number – an important length of time. Number of totality, perfection, completeness times a biblical year.

2,880 - 2,880/8=360 or **8*360=2,880** which is the number of new beginnings times the earth time number. Also a key bridge number connecting the two important earth time numbers 360 and 2,160. It likewise can represent new beginnings.

7,920 – Represents the earth – it is the approximate diameter of the earth in miles – also connects to other earth time numbers – 2,520+2,520+2,520+360=7,920 or 2,160+2,160+2,160+360+360+360+360 =7,920 or 2,520+2,250+2,880=7,920.

10,080 is also a great earth time number. 7,920+2,160=10,080 or 4*2,520=10,080. It represents the earth plus the moon (heavens and earth) or 4 shemitah periods, earth times completion. Of course we can use other combinations of the previous numbers to get this as well.

A quick review: These are God's great earth time numbers.

4 - Earth

72 – Number of years it takes for the equinox line to move 1 degree. Also, 12*6, divine rule times man. (I believe this is also a biblical generation in the context of a measure of time relating to God's master plan of events – an important unit of time as part of God's time clock).

2,160 = 6*360

2,520 = 7*360

HENRY A. RHYNE

2,880 = 8*360

360 – Days in a biblical year, degrees in a sphere – degrees of earth.

365 – Days in a solar year.

7,920 – Approximate diameter of the earth in miles.

10,080 – 7,920+2,160 or 4*2,250.

We also need to make note of any multiples or fractions of these numbers.

At this point I want to suggest the concept of the great earth time clock created by God. All the earth time numbers we have looked at are related to the movement of earth through our solar system. This is like a giant clock created by God – and in the numbers and math of this clock we see cycles that correspond to God's appointed times.

We have two important well known biblical cycles of time – 7 days (6 days and then the 7th day which is the Sabbath day). This is a 7 day cycle.

We also have a 7 year cycle that works the same way - 6 years and then the 7th year is the Sabbath year – called the shemitah year. This 7 year cycle is 2,520 biblical days (7*360).

The 7 year shemitah period is more important than the 7 day period because it is greater in length. Greater length = greater importance. This is the biblical pattern.

I submit that there are far greater cycles of time that are of far greater importance. If 7 days is important and 7 years (2,520 days) is more important than 7 days; then it stands to reason that a period of 2,520 years would be extremely important – far more important than a 7 year period of time.

Therefore, when we see the cycle of 2,520 years ending – meaning the last year in a 2,520 year period we should take notice that it is a very important year, and large biblically prophetic events are likely to happen in that year.

This year ending a 2,520 period is likely to be a super important year in God's plan.

In addition to this there are other large time periods which are biblically important, such as a generation period, a 14 generation period, 70 weeks, 70 weeks of years, 70 generations, 2,160 years (6*360), 2,880 years (8*360).

As you go through this book you will see that many of these larger, super important periods of time are coming together and meeting in one specific year. I believe the year this occurs is 2016, and in 2016 we will see tremendous shaking that is the set up for the last week of years. (The last 7 years aka the tribulation period)

Keep in mind that in Genesis 7:6 we are told Noah was 600 years old when the flood came (6=the number of man). 600 years equals 600*360=216,000. This is a multiple of the 2,160 years it takes for the equinox line to move through a constellation.

Why does God want us to know this? It is interesting that Jesus Christ says that in the last days it will be as in the days of Noah. Could this number be somehow related? We will see this number again.

Before we get to our calculations look at some other important considerations.

BASIC ASTRONOMICAL CONSIDERATIONS

MORE OF THE SECRET ANCIENT KNOWLEDGE OF DANIEL

The earth is 360 degrees around. There are 12 main constellations. As the earth moves in its orbit on any given day we see the sun rise in one of the constellations. It is in each constellation about 30 days – so after one year it is right back where it started. (12 months times 30 days =360 (1 biblical year)).

But, if we look due east on one specific day each year– like the spring equinox we are looking at the sun rising in the same constellation each time year after year.

BTW: Equinox means equal night, the same amount of day and night – equal.

Spring equinox called the Vernal equinox is March 20; the Fall equinox called the Autumnal equinox is September 22. (in the Northern Hemisphere – it is opposite in the Southern Hemisphere).

On these equinox days the sun rises due east and sets due west.

The Bible says that seed time and harvest time will always remain. What is that? It's sowing and reaping (one of God's main kingdom principles); also known as planting and harvesting.

Spring time begins with the spring (Vernal) equinox – it represents the time to plant or the time to sow. Fall begins with the fall (Autumnal) equinox – it represents harvest time – the time to reap.

As a side note: There is an increase in bright meteors in the weeks around the spring equinox. There is debate about whether they are simply more visible at this time of year due to our orbit around the sun or whether at this time of year we enter a debris field so there really are more. In any case more bright meteors are visible at this time of year. Are these signs from God noting the importance of this time of year?

If we look at the sun rise on the spring equinox (we are looking due east) it is in the same constellation year after year, because the earth has completed its yearly orbit so we are right back where we started.

Almost.

Actually we move through the constellations very slowly – meaning the equinox line moves through the constellations very slowly – at the rate of 2,160 years per constellation.

It takes 2,160 years for the equinox line to move through a constellation.

By the way we have (meaning the spring equinox line) just exited Pisces (the fish) and entered Aquarius (the water bearer) in 1990. Most all of Christianity has happened during the time of the fish from 170 BC to 1990 AD.

Earth (360 degrees)

Capricorn

SUN   Aquarius

Due East   Pisces

In the diagram above imagine the horizontal line in the earth is the spring equinox line extending out into the constellation Aquarius – where it is now. Then you can picture this line taking 2,160 years to move through each constellation.

This would mean the equinox line moved 30 degrees.

360/12=30. So, it takes the equinox line 2,160 years to move 30 earth degrees. And 2,160/30=72.

Therefore, it takes the equinox line 72 years to move 1 degree.

There is something very important to point out here. In his book "Finger-Prints Of The Gods", Graham Hancock points out that in various myths and writings the ancients believed that cataclysmic events happened during the period when the equinox line switched from one constellation to the next.

They believed this transition period produced major earth shaking events like an increase in volcano eruptions, earthquakes, floods, extreme weather like ice ages, and an increase in stronger tornadoes and hurricanes, and even destruction from asteroids.

Now this transition period is not just the single year of the change – but this transition period extends for a great many years on either side. So, if this change took place in 1990 the transition period could be a decade or more prior to 1990 and a decade or more after (even a few decades) – because we are dealing with very great lengths of time – 2,160 years – several decades on either side of this is a relatively short time period.

So, the equinox line moving from one constellation to the next is a very big deal – signaling the end of one age and beginning of another. And the cataclysmic events associated with this change mirror many of the descriptions we read about in Revelation and also seem to match some the events we now see taking place around the world today.

We need to look at one more thing then we can start our calculations and unravel the mystery of when Mystery Babylon will fall.

The following is the key that ties everything together – in my research I stumbled on this accidently or possibly divinely. At any rate we will see this is an unusual piece of the puzzle, but it is vital.

An Unlikely Key

More Secret Ancient Knowledge

Daniel would have almost certainly known this.

This key is the simple 3-4-5 Pythagorean triangle.

Further below you will see a 3-4-5 Pythagorean triangle. It is essential in design and has the smallest whole numbers that can work this way.

It is interesting that 3+4+5=12 (the number of divine government).

Why 12 tribes, 12 disciples and 12 main constellations – why not 7 or 8? Is it coincidence or design? I don't believe this a coincidence.

The simple 3-4-5 Pythagorean triangle is the basis for much of modern science and discovery – especially dealing with spheres like the earth and other planets as well as space exploration and all kinds of modern physics. It is essential for space time calculations.

Our universe and solar system is the basis for how we calculate time. We measure time based on the God's great earth time clock which is the universe and solar system.

The universe and solar system is a giant clock – and using mathematics we can tell when the sun will rise and set, where the planets will be at certain times and dates etc.

All of this runs according to mathematical formulas and principles and the 3-4-5 Pythagorean triangle is one of the basic geometric principles and basic formulas that enable us to make these calculations.

In other words the 3-4-5 Pythagorean triangle formula is one of the main roots for much of our modern mathematics relating to time and space.

Therefore, since we are discussing the time when Mystery Babylon will fall and the links in time to the fall of Ancient Babylon, then it makes sense that we would somehow see the Pythagorean triangle related to the timeline of these events.

 A 3-4-5 Pythagorean triangle must meet two conditions in order to be a 3-4-5 Pythagorean triangle.

The sides must be in the 3 to 4 to 5 proportions and it must also fit the equation $A^2+B^2=C^2$.

Below is the 3-4-5 Pythagorean triangle.

$A^2 + B^2 = C^2$ which reads A squared plus B squared equals C squared.

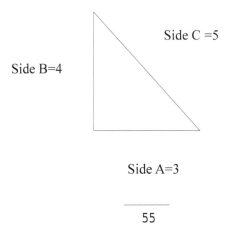

Side C =5

Side B=4

Side A=3

So here we have 9+16=25. Therefore, each of these numbers has importance. Note the result which is 25. The number 25 will come up later.

What if we increase these numbers? What if we make Side C =360?

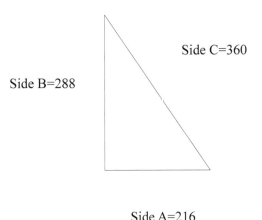

Side C=360

Side B=288

Side A=216

These numbers, 216, 288 and 360 are interconnected.

216 is a fraction of 2,160. 6*360 =2,160, 2,160 is the time for the equinox line to move through a constellation.

360 is the number of degrees in the earth and the days in a biblical year.

288 is a fraction of 2,880 which is 8*360, the number of new beginnings times the earth time number. It is also 12*12*2 or 144*2. Also, if we take the earth number of four and multiply it by 72 (years for the equinox to move one degree) it gives us 288. 4*72=288

Other important earth time numbers are 504 and 25,920 – they are discussed in more detail later on. But for now keep in mind that 216+288 = 504 and 504*360 = 181,440. 181,440/7 = 25,920. 25,920 is the number of years it takes for the equinox line to move through all 12 constellations. (12*2,160 = 25,920) (504 = 360+144) (504*2 = 1,008) (181,440/2016 = 90, 9 = finality)

So, here in the 3-4-5 Pythagorean triangle we see the numbers 216, 288 and 360 - all numbers related to the earth and the great earth time clock – all interconnected. All revealed in the simple Pythagorean triangle.

There are three sides to any triangle including the 3-4-5 Pythagorean triangle – could these three sides represent the Father, Son and Holy Ghost?

"And if one prevail against him, two shall withstand him; and a threefold cord is not quickly broken" (Ecc. 4:12 KJV)

Something that is worth noting is an astronomical formation of three stars called the 'Summer Triangle'. The 'Summer Triangle' is actually visible all year – it consists of the stars Deneb, Vega, and Altair.

This 'Summer Triangle' greatly resembles a 3-4-5 Pythagorean triangle.

I have done crude measurements of it and it is very close to being a 3-4-5 Pythagorean triangle. It is likely impossible to measure with 100% accuracy. However, it is close and in Daniel's day they very well might have considered it to be a 3-4-5 Pythagorean triangle.

So, we could very well have a sign in the stars from Our Creator pointing us to the significance of its' mathematical properties.

What does it all add up to?

Now that we know the basics of the secret ancient knowledge of Daniel we can decipher Daniel's account of the fall of ancient Babylon and find the hidden prophetic message concerning Mystery Babylon.

SOLVING THE MYSTERY

Now we can solve the mystery - the year when Mystery Babylon will Fall.

Ancient Babylon fell in 539 BC.

539/7=77 or 7*77=539.

If Ancient Babylon and Mystery Babylon are connected in time, then the numbers associated with the fall of Ancient Babylon should also be found in relation to the fall of Mystery Babylon.

Since we see the numbers 7 and 77 associated with the year of the fall of ancient Babylon we should also see them related to the year of the fall of Mystery Babylon. (we should also see 2,520 – the number value of the writing on the wall).

The year of the fall of Mystery Babylon should be evenly divisible by 7 as was the year when Ancient Babylon fell.

Remember that every number we involve has to be significant - there can't be any random, meaningless numbers involved or it is not of God.

We have to consider the number 9. The number of finality.

Nothing concerning the biblical end times, meaning the last seven years, can happen until we are in the ninth hour so we need to look after where we see the number 9.

In 1990, on March 20 - we (the spring equinox line) moved from Pisces to Aquarius completing a 2,160 year event. March 20, 2015 was the 25th time this equinox line was in the new constellation (Aquarius).

2015 – 1990 =25 years. 25 years * 360 = 9,000. 9,000 = the final hour.

As of March 20, 2015 we have entered the final hour – or at least this is signaling the final hour is about to begin.

Think about this – the March 20, 2015 solar eclipse happens on the spring equinox and happens in the exact middle of a shemitah year, in the middle of a tetrad of eclipses in which the eclipses fall on Jewish Festival dates and it also just happens to be exactly -
25 years after the spring equinox line switched from being in Pisces to being in Aquarius. It didn't happen in year 23 or 28 or some other year, but in the 25th year. So the math just happens to work out this way. 2015-1990=25. 25*360=9,000. 9,000 – the number representing finality, the 9th hour, the final hour.

I believe that on March 20, 2015 we entered the final week of years as in Daniel's end time prophecy or we are just about to.

So, now we are in the ninth hour and obviously have look after 2015 for the year that Mystery Babylon will fall.

Also, we have to note the blood moons occurring on Jewish festival dates. A lunar eclipse is called a blood moon. 4 full lunar eclipses (blood moons) in a row without a partial lunar eclipse is called a tetrad. Having all blood moons in a tetrad falling on Jewish festivals dates is very rare. But this happens in 2014 – 2015.

The last of the blood moons in this tetrad will happen on September 28, 2015. (September our ninth month). This will complete the tetrad series.

This tetrad is the eighth since the time of Jesus that these blood moons fall on Jewish festival dates. Eight the number of new beginnings.

There are 3 months in 2015 after the tetrad, so could 2015 be the year we see the fall of Mystery Babylon?

I don't think so. 2015/7 = 287.857 - it is not evenly divisible by 7.

539 is evenly divisible by 7 (539/7=77). So, the year of the fall of Mystery Babylon should also be evenly divisible by 7.

How about 2016?

2016/7=288.

2016 is evenly divisible by 7 and it gives us the number 288 which we previously saw has a lot of significance. (288 is a fractional representation of 2,880 = (8*360) which is a new beginning times a biblical year) It also fits the 3-4-5 Pythagorean triangle, and also 4*72 = 288.

So, 2016 certainly is a contender, but we'll need more to confirm this.

If we add 2016 to 539 we get 2,555. We have to add because we are going from BC to AD. 2555 is the number of years from the fall of Ancient Babylon to the year 2016.

Every number has to have significance. Is 2,555 significant in any way? It turns out that it is – in a rather unexpected way.

2016+539=2,555. And 2,555/7=365.

Well, 365 is definitely a significant number – it is the number of our solar year, also the age of Enoch when he was taken by God.

The writing on the wall Daniel interpreted added up to 2,520 which is 7*360, a shemitah period.

2,555 is the number years from the destruction of ancient Babylon to 2016.

2,555*360=919,800 (days).

919,800 days/365=2,520.

This is a direct connection to the destruction of ancient Babylon!

Let's recap where we are now.

Ancient Babylon destroyed in 539 BC. (7*77=539)

The year 2016/7=288

2016+539=2,555.

2555 converts to 2520 (the writing on the wall)

But, what about the number 77?

539/7=77

We should see the number 77 prominently.

And remarkably, we do.

2,555/7=365

2016/7=288

365-288=77.

The last piece of the puzzle has fallen into place.

We have ancient Babylon falling in a year divisible by 7 and connected to the number 77 and to 2,520 and we see the exact same numbers pointing to 2016 as the year Mystery Babylon will fall.

There should be a connection between ancient Babylon and Mystery Babylon in every way. And I believe we have it.

We have the name – Babylon, we have the year 2016 divisible by 7.

We have the length of years from one to the other 2,555, which converts to 2,520 - the number of the writing on wall in Daniel.

We have the significance of 288 related to the great earth time clock.

We have the number 365 – our earth time solar year number.

We have the number 360 – the number of degrees of earth and days in a biblical year.

We have the number 77 by subtracting 288 from 365.

And we have all of this after the number 9. (the number of finality)

2015 is the last year before 2016. In 1990 we ended our time in Pisces and entered Aquarius (the age spoken of by Daniel when he said knowledge would be increased in the last days) 2015-1990=25.

25*360=9000.

A quick summary:

539/7=77.

2016/7=288

539+2016=2555

2555/7=365

365-288=77.

2,555*360 = 919,800

919,800/365 = 2,520

It all adds up and every number is significant. I believe we have solved the mystery.

The great city Mystery Babylon will fall in the year 2016.

And there is this connection to Daniel's last week of years:

2,555*360 = 919,800. 2,520 *360 = 907,200. 919,800 – 907,200 = 12,600. 12,600 is a multiple of the 1,260 days referred to in Daniel. It is three and a half years – a time, times and half a time. So, this is a direct connection to the last week of years. (Daniel 7:25 & 12:7 – also Revelation 12:14)

'As in the days of Noah' – Noah lived 350 years after the flood or 126,000 days.

If that was all we had I believe that would be enough, but there is more.

Here is a further point of interest that adds more even confirmation.

Remember our 3-4-5 Pythagorean triangle? If we make side C = 2,520, then look what we get.

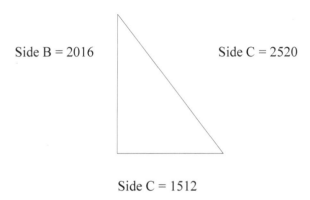

Side B = 2016   Side C = 2520

Side C = 1512

When side C = 2,520 then side B = 2016.

Is this a coincidence? I don't think so.

Here we have a direct relationship between the year 2016 and the number 2,520.

Here is the year 2016 when Mystery Babylon will fall and 2,520 the writing on the wall when Ancient Babylon fell.

1,512 also fits in to the great earth time numbers but less directly.

1,512/7=216 (a fraction of 2,160) a great earth time number. (6*360=2,160) (10,080 = 2,520*4) 2,520-1,512=1,008 a fraction of 10,080. 504*2 = 1,008, 504*3 = 1,512

So, here in the 3-4-5 Pythagorean triangle we see yet another connection between the fall of ancient Babylon and the year 2016 – The year when Mystery Babylon will fall. This is all too much to be coincidence.

About our conversion from 2,555 to 2,520:

Our conversion of 2,555 to 2,520 from Ancient Babylon to Mystery Babylon falling in 2016 gives us a difference of 35 years. (2,555-2,520=35) This difference is necessary to coordinate the different calendars and is also a time of grace. 35=5*7. Grace times completion.

The completion of grace.

And also note that: 2,520/35=72

That great city Mystery Babylon will fall in 2016. When it falls we will know for sure that we are in the last week of years that Daniel prophesied about. This will also mark the beginning of the end of the Babylonian system here on earth and open the door for the return of our Lord Jesus Christ.

Incredibly, there is even more information linking the fall of Mystery Babylon to 2016. And this piece of information not only connects the date but also the location.

THE CITY OF MYSTERY BABYLON IS IN AMERICA

As stated before Mystery Babylon is New York City. NYC is in America. America declared its independence in 1776.

We also know the importance of the number 4 and especially the number 40 (and any multiple of 40).

40 is similar to the wilderness, one is time, the other place – both involve testing, trials, tribulation, but also, God's protection, provision, and blessing. It is where one comes closer to God. One enters earthly, carnal and sinful and either dies or emerges on the other side as heavenly, spiritual, a new creation. (40 can be 4*10, or 5*8)

4 – One enters earthly, comes out heavenly 10 (4*10=40)

5 - One is sustained by God's grace, emerges a new creation 8 (5*8=40)

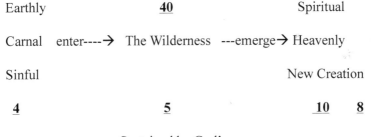

Earthly	40	Spiritual
Carnal enter----→	The Wilderness ---emerge→	Heavenly
Sinful		New Creation
4	**5**	**10** **8**

Sustained by God's grace

40 and the wilderness are the same this way.

We could say 40 = the wilderness.

At its foundation America was a vast wilderness (it was inhabited by Native Americans who were quite vast in number, but the land itself was mostly wilderness).

The Jewish year 5776 runs from September 14, 2015 to October 2, 2016 on our Gregorian solar calendar. So, the Jewish year 5776 takes place primarily in 2016.

For the most part we can say that the Jewish year 5776 = 2016.

America declares its independence in 1776.

5776-1776 = 4,000.

(4,000 = the earth number 4 times 1,000 or 40 times 100) (40 = wilderness, America at its founding = a wilderness) all connected.

This tells us that in 2016 (5776) we will have completed a cycle of 4,000 which is a multiple of 40. This is directly connected to America by the year 1776. This not only confirms the timing of the fall of Mystery Babylon in 2016 – it marks America as the location – it says the city Mystery Babylon resides in America.

This is also confirmed by 2016-1776=240

240*360=86,400

86,400/2,160=40

This completes a 40 period of time.

'As in the days of Noah' – Noah was 600 years old when the flood came, and the rain lasted 40 days.

240/40=6 or 240/6=40

240*360=86,400

86,400/144=600 or 86,400/600=144 (a fraction of the 144,000 sealed in Revelation)

8,640 fits intricately into the great earth time numbers.

8,640/4 = 2,160 – The number 8,640 represents 4 'whole ages'.

8,640/72 = 120 (a multiple of divine rule 12, and also referred to in Genesis 6:3 as the time mankind will rule on earth).

As per Genesis 6:3 120*72=8,640

There are 24 hours in a day. There are 24*60 minutes = 1,440.

There are 24*60*60 seconds = 86,400. We saw above this is also 240*360 = 86,400.

God is great. God's plan is exact down to the very second!

And, these numbers connect to America – as described above.

I'm going to jump the gun a little bit – you will see the importance of these numbers later – but we'll do the calculations here because they fit the subject at hand.

362,880 is an important number.

362,880/86,400 = 4.2

4.2 is a multiple of 42

Three periods of fourteen generations is 42.

Cycles of fourteen generations are very important in God's great timetable (see Matt. 1:17)

3*14 = 42

42 months is also three and a half years (3.5*12=42) (times, time and half a time)

In Revelation we read of the thirds. It takes 25,920 years for the equinox line to move through all 12 constellations. To go through 4 constellations (one-third) takes 8,640 years.

Could God have coordinated the one-thirds in Revelation 8 and 9 with the number 8,640 here – and the equinox line going through one third of the heavenly host? Could they all meet at the same point in time?

2016-1776 = 240

240*360 = 86,400

All of these not only point to the importance of the year 2016, but also the connection of 2016 to America. America is in the Bible and figures into end time events. Israel and America are special because they are the only two nations that had God at their center at their founding. And America has been a tremendous refuge for the Jewish people.

In this I believe we can see the connection of the fall of Mystery Babylon (New York) to America in the year 2016.

As mentioned before the length of time of 2,520 years is super important – a super giant shemitah. If we see this length of time we should take notice. 2016 is the super giant shemitah year – it is the 2,520th year from the fall of Ancient Babylon (by our conversion of 2555).

I firmly believe that not only will we see the fall of Mystery Babylon in 2016, but we will likely see other great prophetic events take place that year as well.

All this is ultimately comes from what is hidden in chapter five in the book of Daniel; Daniel the man of God, prophet, astronomer, and mathematician.

Daniel's account of the fall of Ancient Babylon was not only historic, but also prophetic telling us of the fall of Mystery Babylon.

A 7 year shemitah period is 2,520 days. (7*360 = 2520)

God's pattern would strongly suggest that a 2,520 years period would be of far greater importance than 2,520 days.

If that is correct – and I fully believe it is, then 2016 will be a very eventful period. It is 2,520 years by our conversion from the year when Ancient Babylon fell.

The time from the fall of Ancient Babylon to the year 2016 is one super giant Shemitah period.

I believe this is one of God's great patterns and cycles of time, when earth changing events unfold – like the fall of Ancient Babylon, like Noah's flood etc.

We can expect this period of time to bring about events which will completely alter the direction of mankind. It is very likely this will initiate the tribulation period and rapture – this is the last week of years as recorded in the book of Daniel.

And to conclude this section please beware that 2016 doesn't necessarily mean January to December on our solar calendar. We need to make an allowance for the biblical calendar. So, I would consider the 2016 year to run from September/October 2015 to September/October 2016 – on our solar calendar.

This is the time to watch and it is during this time we will see the words, "Fallen, fallen, that great city has fallen", actually come true.

BEYOND THE CITY OF BABYLON

Could the fall be some year after 2016?

We don't have an unlimited timeline. In Matthew 24, Jesus gives us the parable of the fig tree and says the generation that sees the fig tree bloom will be alive in the last days and at the time of the Great Day of the Lord.

The fig tree is representative of Israel, which was officially formed in 1948. (Trees usually represent nations, or people or peoples – not cities)

This puts a limit on our timeline - of a generation from 1948. What is a generation? I have heard a range suggested from 40 years to 120 years.

60 years would get us to 2008, and that has passed.

I believe a generation is 72 years – the time it takes for the equinox line to move one earth degree, which is also 12*6 = divine rule times man)

Some may say 120 years based on Genesis 6:3. But, that has nothing to do with an individual's life span or generation. We will get to that point later.

Let's use 100 years as a generation just for the sake of argument. So, 100 years plus 1948, means that 2048 is our upper limit of time.

There are only so many years that are evenly divisible by 7 between 2016 and 2048 – so they are really the only other candidates for the fall of Mystery Babylon. All the numbers involved have to be relevant somehow.

77 and 2,520 certainly also have to be involved.

And, there is no other year in this time period where the math adds up the way it does for 2016.

2016 is the only year where the math works like this - where all the numbers involved are relevant and tie together so neatly.

2016 is the year.

Regarding Genesis 6:3 which reads, "And the LORD said, My spirit shall not always strive with man, for that he also is flesh: yet his days shall be an hundred and twenty years." (Gen. 6:3 KJV)

Here God is talking about mankind in general not a specific man – His spirit shall not always strive with mankind. So, God is limiting mankind's time of reign on earth – not an individual's age, therefore this is not a generation.

The Hebrew word for "years" is "sana", which can also mean "whole age". And the word "days" is "yom" which can mean "an indefinite period of time" or "an era with a certain characteristic".

What this verse is saying is that mankind's reign on earth will be 120 ages.

An age is a period of time. So, we can interpret this verse as saying, mankind's reign will be 120 periods of time.

Could this time be related to the time it takes for the equinox line to move through one constellation? I believe so. Perhaps a fraction of that number? 72 years or 2,160 years 120*72=8,640 and 8,640*3=25,920 also 72*360 = 25,920 and 25,920/120 = 216, a fraction of 2,160.

Check out this 3-4-5 Pythagorean triangle:

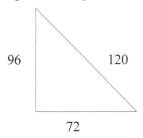

96   120

72

Could the 120 here be the 120 ages in Genesis 6:3 and the 72 the length of those ages?

When side C = 120, side A = 72. Also: 120+72+96 = 288.

In Revelation we read of the thirds – 8,640 is a third of 25,920. (12*2,160= 25,920.) It takes 25,920 years for the equinox line to move through all 12 constellations. Two thirds of the 12 constellations is 8 the number of new beginnings.

We are told in Genesis that Noah was 600 years when the flood came (see Gen. 7:6). 600*360=216,000.

120*2,160=259,200. Or as a fractional representation we get 120*216=25,920, or 12*2,160=25,920

Or we have 120*72=8,640 (8,640 is one third of 25,920)

2,592-2,160=432.

432/2=216.

2*2,160 = 4,320

8*360=2,880

2,880-2,592=288.

Also 2,592-2,520=72

It is all very odd how these numbers are all related to each other and keep coming up over and over again.

If 72 years is a generation then that means there are 25,920 days in a generation (72*360 = 25,920).

Could this be a representation of the 25,920 years it takes for the equinox line to move through all 12 constellations? (12*2,160 = 25,920) (Note: common dominator is 360 degrees)

Could this be connected with mankind's time on earth of 120 periods of time?

120*72 = 8,640. There are 86,400 seconds per day (24*60*60). Could the seconds per day be a representation of mankind's reign on earth?

8,640 * 3 = 25,920 and 3 * 72 = 216 (a fraction of 2,160 years) 120*216 = 25,920.

I believe in Genesis 6:3, God is telling us that the reign of mankind on earth is somehow related to the numbers 120 and 72 or 2,160 and 8,640 or possibly 25,920 or perhaps all of them.

While it is difficult to determine exactly how these connect to Genesis 6:3, it certainly appears they are intricately related to Genesis 6:3.

Here is another interesting twist in connection with 2016.

2016*360 = 725,760. 725,760/8,640 = 84. 84 = 12* 7 (divine rule * completion)

2016*360 = 725,760 and 10,080*72 = 725,760

Side note: 8,640*360 = 3,110,400 and 3,110,400/120 = 25,920

The end of time is fast approaching. The end of mankind's reign on earth as per Genesis 6:3 is near. Soon will be the great day of the LORD and His eternal rule here on earth will begin.

MONTHS OF THE YEAR

When in 2016 will Mystery Babylon fall? What does this mean for America and the world? And how close is this to the rapture?

We can't pinpoint the day – there are too many variables. But, as an educated guess October 2016 is the most likely month. A wise person might look at all of October and perhaps September as well for the fall of Mystery Babylon.

September is our 9ᵗʰ month (9 being the number of finality).

And October is the very next month – right after month nine – Tishri 1 (Rosh Hashanah) will fall on October 3ʳᵈ 2016 and Tishri 16 will fall on October 18ᵗʰ, 2016. Ancient Babylon fell on Tishri 16, (October 12) in 539 BC.

However, we should keep in mind that God can do what He wants when He wants – so we should always be ready.

In the Bible God tells His people to come out of Babylon.

My advice if you are in Mystery Babylon is this: Get out!

We have already discussed what this means for America and the world.

How close is this to the rapture? Well, if you believe in a pre-tribulation rapture then the rapture would occur before this.

I personally believe in a pre-wrath rapture so I believe we will see the fall of Mystery Babylon before the rapture. Exactly how close these two events are I don't know. The fall of Mystery Babylon could be very close to the rapture or years apart – but certainly no more than seven years – and likely no more than three and a half years. But, it will certainly be a significant mark in time and we will then know for sure that we are in the very last of the last days.

5 – 2016: A YEAR UNLIKE ANY OTHER

There are even more interesting attributes concerning the year 2016.

These don't necessarily point to 2016 as being the year Mystery Babylon will fall, but they do point out how the year 2016 is intricately connected to God's great earth time numbers. And, this shows how important the year 2016 is in God's ultimate end time plan and schedule.

In David Flynn's book, 'Temple At The Center Of Time', he points out that 360 is evenly divisible by every single whole number except 7.

Here is the chart.

360/1=360

360/2=180

360/3=120

360/4=90

360/5=72

360/6=60

360/7=51.428571

360/8=45

360/9=40

Look at 360/7 = 51.428571

This is significant because if we drop the decimal point and then multiply (7 * 360 =2,520), we get our earth time number of the shemitah. So, the fact that 360 is not evenly divisible by 7 signals that these two numbers when multiplied are important. This is the pattern.

Well, it just so happens that there is a similar pattern with the number 2016. 2016 is evenly divisible by every single whole number except 5.

Here is the chart.

2016/1=2016

2016/2=1,008

2016/3=672

2016/4=504

2016/5=403.2

2016/6=336

2016/7=288

2016/8=252

2016/9=224

Did you notice some of the results?

Some of the results here are fractions of important earth time numbers – 504, 288, 252 and 1,008.

2016 is evenly divisible by all except for the number 5.

And 5*2016=10,080. This is a very important number, it is 4*2,520. It is also 7,920+2,160.

The earth time number 4 times our 2,520 shemitah number. 4 shemitahs.

It gets stranger.

2016/5=403.2. And 4,032/2=2016. (2 the first number of multiplication or division)

4,032/72=56. The result of 2016 being divided by 5 gives 4,032 (as a multiple), this result divided by 72 (the time it takes for equinox line to move 1 degree = 56), 60-4=56. 60 represents the equinox line moving through two constellations, less our earth number four gives 56.

56 is also 8*7 (new beginnings multiplied by completion) and 56/72 = .7777777 repeating.

4,032-2016=2016.

2,520-2016=504.

360+144=504. (earth time number plus 144 (represents the 144,000 sealed in revelation) – also 72*2=144)

2,160-2016=144.

2016/72=28, and 28=4*7 or 4 (number of earth) shemitah periods.

2160+2160 = 4,320

2016/5=403.2

4,320-4,032 = 288 (288 as a fraction of 2,880 = 8*360), New beginning times the earth number and as part of our 3-4-5 Pythagorean triangle.

2016 AND THE END OF TIME

2016/8 (number of new beginnings) = 252 (a fraction of 2,520)

The numerical sequence 1,2,3,4,5,6,7,8,9 is very important. With these numbers we can calculate all numbers. By using addition, subtraction, multiplication and division we can get any number that exists. There is no number that can't be derived from this sequence of numbers.

This sequence therefore represents all numbers. This sequence also represents time – ALL OF TIME from beginning to end – in an appointed period of time – a complete age – an age of God.

1 – The beginning through 9 – the end (finality)

"Hearken unto me, O Jacob, and Israel, my called; I am he; I am the first, I also am the last." (Is. 48:12 KJV)

"Saying, I am Alpha and Omega, the first and the last: …" (Rev.1:11 KJV)

There are many other verses in which the LORD God refers to Himself as the first and the last.

So, it makes sense that sequence 1,2,3,4,5,6,7,8,9 would be very important.

Our great earth time number of 360 doesn't just represent the earth. There are 360 degrees in a sphere – in earth. So, this number 360 represents the fullness of the earth. (BTW: 360/90=40)

If we divide 360 by the first number of multiplication or division 2 we get 180 – representing the fullness of the earth divided.

If we take the beginning number of the sequence 1 and add it to the end number 9, we get 10. 10 representing heaven. The beginning and the end equals heaven. The number 10 is a heavenly multiplier. (the tithe is a tenth, the 10 commandments) 10*4(earth) = 40 which of course we see in regards to the journey toward God. 40 is the period of transition from one period to the next.

THE SECRET ANCIENT CODE OF DANIEL

1*2*3*4*5*6*7*8*9 = 2*3*4*5*6*7*8*9 because 1 does not multiply.

The first number of multiplication 2 times the end 9 = 18. 18 is a fractional representation of 180. 18*10=180.

So, 180 comes from the first number of multiplication in this sequence times the end number, times the first plus the last. (2*9) * (1+9) = 180.

180 is half of 360, so 180 represents earth divided or a divided earth.

Note: The number 10 can be thought of as Heaven or God's Kingdom.

ALL OF TIME IN AN AGE

1*2*3*4*5*6*7*8*9 represents all of time in an age (from 1 the beginning to 9 the end) and equals 362,880.

So likewise 362,880 represents all of time in an age, from beginning to end – from the first to the last. (1 through 9)

362,880 divided by 180 = 2016. (362,880/180 = 2016) or (362,880/2016 = 180)

All of time divided by a divided earth = 2016. Or we could say, all of time divided by 2016 = a divided earth.

Also, 2,520*144=362,880

A shemitah multiplied by the 144 representing those sealed in Revelation = 362,880 or 362,880/2,520 = 144. A complete age from beginning to end divided by the shemitah equals the 144 (as in Revelation). As we saw 2016 is the 2,520th year from the fall of ancient Babylon (by our conversion).

1*2*3*4*5*6*7*8*9 = 362,880 both therefore represent all of time – from beginning to end – in a complete age.

In Matthew 1:17 we read of the three 14 generation periods from Abraham to Christ. I believe a generation is 72 years – the time it takes for the equinox line to move 1 degree and it is also 12*6 (divine rule times man).

Using 72 years as a generation then:

One 14 generation period then equals 14*72*360 = 362,880.

Recap: 1*2*3*4*5*6*7*8*9=362,880

2,520*144=362,880

14*72*360=362,880

180*2016=362,880

362,880/360 = 1,008 (a fraction of 10,080)

10,080= 4*2,520

10,080/2016 = 5 (grace)

or 5*2016= 10,080

Also 2016/2 =1,008

1,008*10 =10,080

362,880 represents all of time in an age, 360 represents the fullness of earth, so 1,008 is all of time divided by the fullness of earth, 1,008 is the result of time divided by a full earth. (362,880/360 = 1,008) 1,008*10 = 10,080

And this result divided by the year 2016 = 5, the number of grace. (10,080/2016=5)

I believe the interpretation is that in 2016 grace has run out – at this point we have passed grace.

In the first chapter of Matthew we have the genealogy of Christ and part reads as follows: "So all the generations from Abraham to David are fourteen generations; and from David until the carrying away into Babylon are fourteen generations; and from the carrying away into Babylon unto Christ are fourteen generations." (Matt. 1:17 KJV)

Here we can obviously see the importance of the number 14 and especially the importance of 14 generations.

$362,880/14 = 25,920$.

This is interesting because 25,920 is the time it takes for the equinox line to move through all 12 constellations.

This links to the year 2016.

$2016*360 = 725,760$

$362,880*2 = 725,760$

And as we saw, $362,880/360 = 1,008$ – a fraction of 10,080.

This is also $4*2,520$, or $5* 2016$ or the earth number 7,920 plus the moon number 2,160 ($7,920+2,160 = 10,080$) Earth and moon represent heaven and earth.

In Matthew 1:17 if we count each of the generations as 72 years (the time it takes for the equinox line to move one degree);

then for one 14 generation period we get $14*72 = 1,008$.

The number of Godly divine rule 12, times the number of man 6 = 72 ($12*6 = 72$) so, I believe this is the years in a generation.

Each of the three 14 generation periods equals 1,008. (14*72 = 1,008) 1,008 years is one 14 generation period.

3 of these periods take us from the time of Abraham to the time of Christ. 3*14*72 = 3,024 years.

From the time of Christ to 2016 we have 2016/72=28 (generations).

28 = 2*14. So, from the time of Christ to 2016 we have 2 periods of fourteen generations. 2*14*72=2016

The total then, from the time of Abraham (who was under grace not law) to the year 2016 is 5 periods of fourteen generations. 5 is the number of grace. Beyond the year 2016 we are entering the 6th 14 generation period from Abraham – 6 is the number of man. 666 is the number of the anti-Christ.

I believe this is further confirmation saying that grace runs out in the year 2016. By this I mean for the world, not for the saints. For the saints I believe are always under grace. But, for the world the period of grace is about to run out – 2016 will bring the fall of Mystery Babylon, the start of the collapse of the Babylonian system, and the tribulation period beginning as signaled by the equinox on March 20, 2015.

Noah is the 10th from Adam and Abraham is the 10th from Noah.

From Adam to Abraham people lived much longer – so a generation back then is different from a generation from Abraham forward. We can't compare generations prior to Abraham to those after in the same lengths of time – it is not an apples to apples comparison.

I believe this is why in Matthew 1 we only see the genealogy of Christ beginning with Abraham. Things changed with Abraham – Abraham being called was the new beginning of God's kingdom on earth (Genesis chapter 12) as opposed to the Babylonian kingdom started by Nimrod (Genesis chapter 10).

We have two periods of time prior to Abraham, but the number of generations is not known at this time. I can't prove it, but I believe the pre Abraham time period is 50 generations (of 72 years); in the context of Genesis 6:3 – where God limits mankind's age to 120 periods of time – note it was in Noah's time when God made this decree.

In other words the pre - Abraham period of time is the equivalent of 50 generations (of 72 years). 50 is a multiple of 5, which is grace and Abraham was under grace. Keep in mind that in Genesis 6:3 God says mankind's time on earth will be 120 generations (using a generation as a period of time).

At this point I can't definitely prove the pre-Abraham time is 50 generations.

But, we do know the generations from Abraham to Christ are 42. There are three 14 generation periods.

(BTW: 3.5 years is 42 months as in Daniel and Revelation – God's numerical patterns are consistent)

If we use 72 years as a generation then 14 generations is 1,008 years. Peter tells us that a day with the LORD is as 1,000 years, and 1,000 years as a day.

Could this actually be 1008 years? (14*72 = 1,008)

2016/72=28

We have 42 generations from Abraham to Christ and from Christ to the year 2016 is 28 generations. This gives us 42+28=70.

That means we have 70 generations from Abraham to the year 2016!

2016 is the end of the 70th generation from the time of Abraham.

70 is super important. It is completeness times heaven - God's Kingdom. It is 10 shemitah generation periods – and it ends in 2016.

70 Generations and 70 weeks of years

Could this 70 generations from Abraham to 2016 correspond to the 70 weeks of Daniel?

I believe so. The ending of the 70 generations from the time of Abraham will collide with the 70th week of years per Daniel – in 2016.

I will comment more on Daniel's 70 weeks a little further on – but now look at this.

86,400 seconds per day (24*60*60 = 86,400)

8,640 is a third of 25,920 – the time it takes for the equinox line to move through all 12 constellations. We read of the one thirds in Revelation 8 & 9.

Abraham to Jesus Christ is 42 generations = **3,024 years.**

Jesus Christ to 2016 is 28 generations = **2,016 years.**

Abraham to 2016 is 70 generations = **5,040 years.**

Genesis 6:3 – 120 generations from the time of Noah (pre Abraham).

120 generations less 70 generations = 50 generations.

50 generations times 72 = **3,600 years** (pre – Abraham) (note this is 360*10)

3,600+3,024+2,016 = 8,640. (Ending in the year 2016)

Back to Abraham:

Abraham was under grace – Could that period of grace end after 70 generations? (7 means completion and 70 = 10*7 or God's Kingdom times completion)

70 generations * 72yrs each * 360 = 1,814,400

This is five 14 generation periods of time (5*14*72*360 = 1,814,400).

1,814,400/362,880=5 (grace)

I believe the grace period ends in 2016 for the world – the saints I believe will always be under grace.

Also, 1,814,400/2016 = 900 (9 is finality, 9th hour the final hour)

In the section with the 3-4-5 Pythagorean triangle we saw a fraction of 1,814,400. We saw 181,440 = 504*360 and also 72*2,520 = 181,440.

And here we see a multiple connected to 2016.

The wedding in Cana takes place on the third day – a prophetic foreshadow of when the Bridegroom Christ takes His saints as His Bride – the wedding. (See John 2)

If one day = 1,008 years, then 2016 would be the end of the second day and the end of 2016 would be the beginning of the prophetic third day when the wedding takes place. (2016/2 = 1,008) Prophetically, 2016 would be the very end of the second day - midnight. The next day is the wedding day. This raises the question – how early in the third day does the wedding take place?

This, I don't know, but I believe it will be very early in the morning. In the parable of the ten virgins – the LORD comes very early, at midnight, meaning very soon after the second day turns into the third day.

Converting years into days or days into years, I believe we will see the return of the LORD within a couple of years of 2016.

I believe the autumn of 2018 which is 3.5 years after the spring equinox on March 20, 2015 is the most likely season. The autumn of 2018 is very soon after the year of 2016. In terms of thousands of years, it represents minutes. (Actually it represents 5 minutes – 5 – the number of grace).

1,008 years/24 hours = 42

42 years / 60 minutes = .7 years per minute

Three and a half years (as in Daniel) /.7 years = 5 minutes.

God is awesome.

Further consideration is the three periods of 14 generations from Abraham to Christ which equals 3*14*72 = 3,024 years. The time from Christ to the year 2016 is 2016 years – approximately (2*14*72 = 2016). 3,024+2,016 = 5,040.

5,040/360 = 14.

362,880 represents all of time from beginning to end (1 through 9 as 1*2*3*4*5*6*7*8*9) as a complete age.

Also: 14*72*360=362,880

I believe that 2016 completes this number.

From Abraham to the year 2016 is 5 periods of fourteen generations of 72 years. (5*14*72 = 5,040)

362,880/5,040 = 72

From Abraham to the year 2016 = 5,040 years. (70 generations *72 years per generation)

5,040/72 = 70. (10 (heaven) shemitahs)) – ten heavenly shemitahs – 70 generations, 70 weeks

5,040/2 = 2,520 (a 7 year shemitah period and the writing on the wall)

2,520-2016=504 (a fraction of 5,040)

Counting from Abraham to the year 2016 is 5,040 years.

One 14 period of generations = 14*72 = 1,008 (a fraction of 10,080)

2016/1,008 = 2

5,040/1,008 = 5 (grace)

Grace from Abraham to the year 2016 – then grace is over.

6 - MORE ABOUT 2016

The significance of the year 2016 goes even deeper.

362,880 represents all of time as 1 through 9 multiplied. (beginning to end) or it represents all of the time in an age or in a cycle of time.

362,880 times the first number of multiplication 2 = 725,760

$362,880*2 = 725,760$

$2016*360 = 725,760$

The second Jewish temple was destroyed in 70 AD.

$2016-70 = 1946$

$2016*360 = 725,760$

$1946*360 = 700,560$

$725,760 - 700,560 = 25,200$ (a multiple of 2,520)

$2016*360 = 725,760$

$725,760/2,520 = 288$

(288 is a fraction of 2,880, a number of new beginnings as $2,880 = 8*360$)

$362,880/2,520 = 144$ (144 is $12*12$ or $72*2$) - a fraction of the 144,000 sealed in Revelation.

We know from Matt. 1:17 14 generations is an important length of time in God's timetable of events. Major events happen on these cycles.

If 72 is a generation then a 14 generation cycle of time in days would be $14*72*360 = 362,880$.

This means that 2016 is the year that marks the end of a 14 generation cycle of time – actually from Christ to 2016 would be 2 cycles of 14 generations of time. 2016*360=725,760. 725,760/2=362,880. The second cycle of this length of time ends in 2016.

Watch for incredibly major events to take place in 2016, in addition to the fall of Mystery Babylon.

362,880/14 = 25,920.

This is the length of time it takes for the equinox line to move through all 12 main constellations. 12*2,160=25,920; and a 14 generation is an important biblical length of time.

2016/14 = 144

And 362,880/2,520 = 144

In Daniel chapter 9 we are told of the 70 weeks of years.

These are divided into a period of 69 weeks of years, then an interval, and then the last week of years. We have been in this interval between the 69th and the 70th year for a long time. Now, I believe we are finally entering the final 70th week of years – at the same time we are ending the 70th generation from Abraham.

2016*360=725,760

69 weeks of years = 69*7*360 = 173,880

725,760-173,880=551,880

551,880/2,160=255.5 (255.5 is a fraction of 2555)

2555 is 2016 + 539 (the year Ancient Babylon fell)

2016/2=1,008 (1,008 is a fraction of 10,080)

10,080 = 4*2,520

10,080 also is 7,920+2,160 (the earth number plus the moon number representing the heavens and earth)

2016*360=725,760

725,760/2=362,880

362,880-173,880 (Daniel's 69 weeks) =189,000

189,000/2,520=75

2016-2001=15 (2016 is 15 years from 9/11)

15*360=5,400 which represents the time from 9/11 to 2016.

5,400/72=75

I believe Jesus Christ died on the cross in 33 AD as per Rick Larson's DVD 'The Star of Bethlehem'. In this DVD Larson presents convincing evidence of the date of the cross as being in 33 AD.

2016-33=1983

1983*360=713,880

69 weeks of years of Daniel = 173,880 (7*360*69=173,880)

Notice all the numbers are the same – but the arrangement is different.

713,880-173,880 = 540,000 (this is a multiple of 5,400) which is interconnected with all the great earth time numbers.

10,080 -5,400=4,680, (10,080 = 4*2,520) (7,920+2,160=10,080) (5*2016 = 10,080) (14*72=1,008)

4,680=2,160+2,520

As David Flynn notes in his book, 'Temple At The Center of Time', When Joshua marched around the city of Jericho before it fell he went around (360 degrees) once a day for six days (6*360=2,160), then on the 7th day he went around seven times (7*360=2,520). In total he went around the city 2,160+2,520=4,680. 4,680 + 5,400 = 10,080.

5,400-2,520=2,880

2,520+2,520+360=5,400

2,160+2,160+360+360+360=5,400

540,000 divided by the number of finality 9 = 60,000 (a multiple of 6 – the number of man)

Noah was 600 years old when the flood came.

600*9 (finality) =5,400 (a fraction of 540,000)

All linked to 2016 and Daniel's 69 weeks from above 2016-33 = 1983

2*2,160 = 4,320 This represents 2 ages – the equinox line moving through two constellations

540*8 (new beginnings) = 4,320

As Graham Hancock notes in his book, 'Finger-Prints of the Gods', this number 4,320 is incorporated in the pyramids in South America by using the numbers 540 and 80 (540*80=43,200). It is also incorporated in the great pyramid of Giza in Egypt. There are some who think that the pyramid is a model of the Northern Hemisphere with the point as the pole and the perimeter as the equator. Amazingly, in this light the pyramid is almost perfectly built to the scale of 1 to 432,000.

In Revelation 21: starting in verse 10 we see the city of new Jerusalem descending out of heaven. The sides – width and depth and the height are all equal. These are the dimensions of a pyramid.

I believe that the fallen angels, the nephelim (giants) and their offspring were instrumental in the building of the pyramids. Why a pyramid shape? They were trying to replicate something they saw in heaven before they fell. So, the fact that the number 4,320 shows up in both, one by scale and the other by way of 540 and 8 being built into them is very significant. These are numerical connections with the dimensions given in Revelation, the pyramids and the great earth time numbers.

So, when we take $2016 - 33 = 1983$ and then $1983*360 = 713,880$ and Daniel's 69 weeks of years = 173,880; then the difference is $713,880 - 173,880 = 540,000$ it reveals a deep connection of God's great earth time numbers and ultimately the year 2016; And also it is a connection between 9/11/2001 and the year 2016.

And then there is this:

$2016*360 = 725,760$

$725,760/2,520 = \mathbf{288}$

$173,880/2,520 = \mathbf{69}$

$725,760 - 173,880 = 551,880$

$551,880/2,520 = \mathbf{219}$

$288 + 69 + 219 = 576$

576 (divided by our earth time number 72 – also a generation) = 8 (the number of new beginnings)

$576/72 = 8$ and $2*288 = 576$

The fact that we see 288+69+219=576 in relation to 2016 and Daniel's 69th week of years is significant. 576 also fits in a 3-4-5 Pythagorean triangle combined with other earth time numbers. I believe this signals the end of the interval between the 69th and 70th week.

When the 4 side = **576**, the 3 side = **432** and the 5 side = **720** which is 2*360 (or 10*72)

We have already noted 432 as 4,320 (2*2,160) and 432,000 in relation to the pyramids.

576+432 = 1,008 and 720*1,008 = 725,760 = 2016*360 which is yet another connection between Daniel's 69 weeks of years and 2016 – I believe this tells us that in 2016 the 70th week begins.

2016-576=1,440 (a multiple of 144)

576 is a fraction of 5,760

5,760/2=2,880

576/144=4

Three and a half years is a time, times and half a time as referred to in Daniel and Revelation regarding the last days.

288+69+219=576 (from the above calculation)

2016/576 = 3.5 – Another connection to Daniel's 70 weeks of years.

Daniel's 69 weeks of years = 173,880 (69*7*360).

Ancient Babylon fell in 539 BC.

539*360=194,040.

194,040 – 173,880 = 20,160 (a multiple of 2016) – Yet another connection to Daniel's 70 weeks of years and again linked to 2016.

If March 20, 2015 is the beginning of the last week of seven years then it would conclude in 2022. And the new beginning would be 2023. Or if we use the Biblical year we could run into the year 2023.

Or 2016+7 = 2023.

2023*360=728,280

728,280-725,760=2,520

2023-33(year of the cross) =1990

1990 is the year the equinox line moved into a new constellation completing a 2,160 year cycle.

8 represents new beginnings.

2016*5=10,080

10,080/8 = 1,260 (as in Daniel)

2016/8=252 (a fraction of 2,520)

The sequence 1,2,3,4,5,6,7,8 represents time from the beginning to a new beginning.

1*2*3*4*5*6*7*8 = 40,320.

A fractional representation of this is 403.2

2016 is evenly divisible by every number except 5 (grace)

2016/5 = 403.2

Or 403.2*5 = 2016

Here we have grace and new beginnings in relationship with the number 2016.

12 (The number of Kingdom rule) * 360 the number of the fullness of the earth equals 4,320 which is also, 2*2,160

4320-4032 = 288. 288 is a fraction of 2880. (8*360) so, 288 is a representation of new beginnings.

2016/288 = 7

2016 divided by new beginnings equals completion

2016/5=403.2

362,880/40,320 = 9

2016*360=725,760

725,760/40,320=18 (18=2*9)

9 = finality

As we saw earlier 4 shemitah periods = 10,080. (7*360 = 2,520) and (4*2,520 = 10,080) 4 is the number of earth. 10,080 is also the diameter of the earth plus the diameter of the moon in miles (approximately) - which represents heaven and earth. (7,920+2,160)

72 is a generation (12*6) Divine rule times the number of man – also the time for the equinox line to move 1 degree.

725,760 = 2016. (2016*360)

725,760/72 = 10,080. Or 72*10,080 = 725,760.

7 - A LAST WORD ON 2016

Background: I believe Jesus died on the cross in 33 AD

The Equinox line moved into a new constellation in 1990

2016 is most likely the start of the last week of years as per Daniel.

2016-33 = 1983

$$\underline{1983} \ldots\ldots\ldots\ldots\ldots\ldots +40 \ldots\ldots\ldots\ldots\ldots\ldots = \underline{2023}$$

$$+ 7 = 1990 \qquad\qquad -7 = 2016$$

1990 (Equinox line)

2023 (possible end of tribulation and wrath – the end of time – new heaven and new earth)

2016 (probable start of tribulation period – the last 7 years)

A PECULIAR PIECE OF AMERICAN HISTORY

Solomon Pietersen was one the first official Jews in America. He came from Brazil, known then as the 'Land of The Holy Cross' to New Amsterdam in the wilderness of America.

Solomon Pietersen comes from the land of the Holy Cross to America in 1654.

2 years later in 1656 he married a Christian woman – the first official recognized interfaith marriage of Jew and Christian in America.

1656 + 360 = 2016

Coming full circle (360) from the first official interfaith marriage between Jew and Christian in 1656 brings us to 2016.

So, what does all this mean?

2016 is unlike any other year.

It means that the year 2016 is intimately linked to all the great earth time numbers. 2016 fits into all of God's great numbers in a way that is unlike others. 2016 is extremely unique. And 2016 also fits in with American history.

2016 is deeply connected to God's great end time plan and 2016 is connected to America.

2016 is highly significant in God's great plan and His great earth time clock, which was created at the very beginning, and tells us the season we are in.

2016 marks the end of a great, giant cycle of time.

2016 is a marker of time in God's great plan.

In 2016 we will see the convergence of many important time cycles.

Message for the year 2016: Stay Awake and WATCH.

The Jerusalem Connection

We see Israel as the fig tree in the parable Jesus tells us in Matthew 24.

However, Jerusalem is also a special place on earth. It is the Holy city, it is the city that Jesus laments for, and God is going to create a New Jerusalem.

"Nevertheless I must walk today, and tomorrow, and the day following: for it cannot be that a prophet perish out of Jerusalem.

O Jerusalem, Jerusalem, which killest the prophets, and stonest them that are sent unto thee; how often would I have gathered thy children together, as a hen doth gather her brood under her wings and ye would not! Behold, your house is left unto you desolate: and verily I say unto you, Ye shall not see me, until the time come when ye shall say, BLESSED IS HE THAT COMETH IN THE NAME OF THE LORD." (Luke 13:33-35 KJV)

"But I say unto you, Swear not at all; neither by heaven for it is God's throne: Nor by the earth; for it is his footstool; neither by Jerusalem; for it is the city of the great king". (Matt. 5:34-35 KJV)

"Him that overcometh will I make a pillar in the temple of my God, and he shall go no more out: and I will write upon him the name of my God, and the name of the city of my God, which is new Jerusalem, which cometh down out of heaven from my God: and I will write upon him my new name." (Rev. 3:12 KJV)

The Holy Bible refers to Jerusalem 811 times. (KJV)

In 1948 the nation of Israel was established. Jerusalem was reclaimed in 1967 as a result of the six day war.

2016-1967=49

From the year Jerusalem was reclaimed to the year 2016 is 7 periods of 7. This length of time is a shemitah times a shemitah or 7 shemitahs. It is 7 sets of 7 years. (perfection, totality, completeness times perfection, totality, completeness)

It is rather incredible how these numbers concerning Jerusalem just happen to add up this way in the year 2016 – where we saw all the other mathematical calculations also point to 2016.

So, here we have another large shemitah period ending in the year 2016. One super giant shemitah period from the fall of Ancient Babylon to 2016, and the other from the reclamation of Jerusalem in 1967. And from Abraham to 2016 is 10 shemitah generation periods. We have 70 generations from Abraham to 2016 and Daniel's 70th week of years all meeting in the year 2016 – which is also deeply connected to God's great earth time numbers.

I think it is important to reemphasize the following point.

Earlier we did the calculation to measure from the Fall of Ancient Babylon to the year 2016.

It was calculated as follows:

2016+539=2,555.

2,555*360=919,800.

919,800/365=2,520

Thus 2,555 converts to 2,520.

The difference is 35. (2,555-2,520=35)

2,520/35=72

Here we see the shemitah period of 2,520 divided by our difference in the conversion equaling the amount of time it takes for the equinox line to move one degree or the years in a generation (72=12*6)

35=5*7, here it is years, so 35 represents five shemitah periods or grace times the shemitah.

I submit that this 35 year difference period (5*7) (5 shemitah periods of time) represents a grace timeout period. (5 – the number of grace times the number of completion 7). Grace times completion – means that a cycle of grace has been completed.

This period was necessary to coordinate the biblical and solar calendars and it was an extension of God's grace before the tribulation period.

In 2016 this time out period is over.

Again, keep in mind we are operating with two calendars, so 2016 may not necessarily be our January to December, but could possibly be September / October 2015 to September / October 2016.

Personally I believe that the solar 2016 (January to December) is more likely since this is the calendar we are on now. But, the possibility of the timing being coordinated with the biblical calendar and year needs to be recognized.

Again, many thanks to Graham Hancock and David Flynn for their books, 'Finger Prints of the Gods' and 'Temple at the Center of Time', respectively.

If you are interested this sort of study and information, I highly recommend their two books.

Their two books were the genesis of this discovery, from there the spirit of the Lord took over and the result was this revelation.

888 – JESUS THE CHRIST

888 is the number of Jesus Christ.

At first glance it doesn't appear that 888 is connected to any of the numbers we have studied. 888 is not evenly divisible by 72 or 360 – and the fractions don't seem relevant. 2,160, 2,520 and 10,080 are not evenly divisible by 888 and again the fractions seem irrelevant.

On the other hand we would expect the number of Jesus to be connected with everything, just because it is the number of Jesus.

Well, actually the number of Jesus Christ does connect to the great earth time numbers, America and Daniel's 70 weeks of years.

America declares its independence in 1776.

888*2 = 1776 (2 - the first number of multiplication)

888*72 = 63,936

63,936/360 = 177.6

I believe this shows how supernatural the forming of the U.S. was. God was fundamentally involved in the very forming of America. (The following connects this to the year 2016 - as significant)

2016 – 1776 = 240

2016*360 = 725,760 (Note: this is two 14 generation periods from the time of Jesus Christ)

888*360 = 319,680 (we multiply this by 2 for the two 14 generation periods)

319,680*2 = 639,360

725,760 – 639,360 = 86,400

240*360 = 86,400

Also, note that 86,400/2,160 = 40

And 86,400 is the number of seconds per 24 hour day. (24*60*60 = 86,400)

86,400/12 = 7,200

Here we see the number of Jesus tied to the great earth time numbers and America.

Of course it goes deeper.

$888*360 = 319,880$

$362,880$ is one 14 generation period which is also $1*2*3*4*5*6*7*8*9$

$362,880 - 319,880 = 43,200$

$2*2,160 = 4,320$ (a tenth of 43,200)

$888*72 = 63,936$

$63,936*360 = 23,016,960$

$23,016,960/888 = 25,920$ (this is the equinox line going through all 12 constellations – a full cycle $12*2,160 =25,920$)

Daniels 70 weeks of years = $70*7*360 = 176,400$

$888*360 = 319,680$

$319,680 - 176,400 = 143,280$

$143,280/72 = 1990$

72 is the years it takes for the equinox line to move 1 degree – also a generation – $12*6 = 72$ (divine rule times man)

1990 is the year when the equinox line moved into a new constellation after 2,160 years (170 BC to 1990 AD)

And of course $2015-1990 = 25$ and $25*360 = 9,000$ (9 finality, the 9th hour is the final hour)

So, here we see the number Jesus connected to the final hour signaled in 2015 and the 70 weeks of Daniel.

1990, (9/11)2001 AND 2016

9/11 happened in the 9th month of the year - 9 = finality, during the month of the Autumnal Equinox. This is the 11th year the Autumnal Equinox line would be in the constellation of Leo (The Lion).

Here is a quick review of the meaning of some numbers.

7,920 represents the fullness of the earth. (approximate dimension of the earth in miles).   This is also 22*360. (11 is half of 22; 22/2 = 11) and 7,920/2 = 3,960

2,160 represents one earth age – it is the time it takes for the equinox line to move through a constellation and it is also the approximate diameter of the moon in miles.

7,920+2,160 = 10,080, which is 4 shemitah periods (4*2,520 = 10,080), also represented as 4*7 = 28. 28*360=10,080

180 represents the fullness of the earth divided – as 360 also represents the fullness of the earth – 360 years in a Biblical year and 360 degrees of the sphere of earth. (360/2=180)

11 represents chaos – it is between 10 heaven – God's Kingdom, and 12 divine rule. It is something added to heaven yet short of God's divine rule. It is 7+4. A shemitah plus the earth.

1990 is our starting point because that is when the equinox lines (vernal and autumnal) moved into new constellations completing a cycle of 2,160 years.

2001 – 1990 = 11 (chaos) 11 = 7+4 (shemitah plus the earth)

$11*360 = 3,960$

$3,960 - 2,520 = 1,440$ or $2,520+1,440 = 3,960$ (shemitah plus the 144,000 sealed in Revelation) 1,440 is a fractional representation of 144,000. In Genesis we are told mankind's reign shall be 120 years (ages) $12*120 = 1,440$

$1,440/360 = 4$ or $4*360=1,440$

So, 3,960, is the time from 1990 to 9/11 = 3,960 which = a shemitah (2520) + (4*360) One earth number times another earth number.

$2001-1990 = 11$ $(11*360=3,960)$

7,920 (fullness of the earth) divided by 2 (first number of division) = 3,960. $(7920/2 = 3960)$ The fullness of the earth divided = 3,960. 3,960 represents the time from 1990 to 2001.

$3,960 - 2,160$ (one earth age) = 1,800. 1,800 is a multiple representation of 180. 360 as the fullness of the earth / 2 =180. So, 180 represents the fullness of the earth divided.

The time from 1990 to 2001 = one earth age (the 2,160 cycle ending in 1990), then the fullness of the earth divided, 1,800 as a multiple of 180)

I believe this numerical connection is by design and it further reveals to us the location of Mystery Babylon as New York City and 2016 as the year it will fall.

We should also take note of 2015 especially September and October. September 2015 is 14 years after 2001.

14 is of course significant – it is $2*7$ or $2*2,520 = 5,040$ And 5,040 is half of 10,080.

$14*360=5,040$

$5,040/72=70$

Remember the important scripture of Matt. 1:17 concerning the birth of Jesus Christ. "So all the generations from Abraham to David are fourteen generations; and from David until the carrying away into Babylon are fourteen generations; and from the carrying away into Babylon into Babylon unto Christ are fourteen generations."

Here we see the importance of fourteen generations (Fourteen generation periods). Years and generations are connected. So, a fourteen year period can be a representation of a fourteen generation period.

Biblically speaking, major events happen on these fourteen generation cycles as mentioned in the scripture above.

The towers falling in 2001 was obviously a major event with Biblically prophetic implications and as Jonathan Cahn notes in his book, 'The Harbinger', it is a replaying of warning events that occurred in Ancient Israel.

2015 and 2016 are both important years regarding New York aka New Amsterdam aka Mystery Babylon.

And therefore both are very important for America and for the end times.

MYSTERY BABYLON HAS FALLEN

How is Mystery Babylon likely to fall?

The top candidate is a nuclear event.

Ancient Babylon was toppled by an enemy, so that is the top Biblical pattern.

The Middle East is heating up with warfare. The rise of Islam and radical Islamic groups is creating great turmoil. There is a lot of brutality against Christians and Jews. These radical Islamic groups want to destroy Christians and Jews and they are clear about that. Many of them consider America to be the great Satan and Israel to be the little Satan.

At present time Iran is seeking and pursuing a nuclear weapon and they are very close to making this a reality. Iran has been pursuing a nuclear weapon for decades and has gone to extraordinary lengths to achieve nuclear capability. Why go to such extremes for so long for a weapon of mass destruction? It is not for defensive purposes. No nation presents an existential threat to Iran.

Iran has also routinely sponsored Islamic terrorists for years, many who themselves have sought to obtain nuclear weapons to use against the U.S. and Israel.

If Iran and/or these radical Islamic groups get a nuclear weapon, what will they do with it? I believe if they get a nuclear weapon they will almost immediately use it. Understand this is not about politics or economics – it is about their religious belief. Assuming Iran and or these groups get nuclear weapons I believe we will see two events soon after – a nuclear attack on America specifically New York City and also a nuclear attack on Israel. These actions will fulfill prophecy (the destruction of Mystery Babylon) and start a cascade of more events that will also fulfill end time prophecies.

I believe this nuclear attack is the most likely way we will see the destruction of Mystery Babylon take place.

On a recent news program, I heard one of the commentators stating that nuclear weapons today are many times larger and more powerful than the bomb dropped on Hiroshima. This person said some nuclear weapons today are 3,000 to 5,000 times more powerful.

This is almost inconceivable. But, in any event if a bomb as strong as the one dropped on Hiroshima or a little bit stronger impacted New York its effects would reach much farther. New York (Mystery Babylon) would be destroyed by the direct impact. The indirect impact could reach a wider area – maybe from Washington, DC. to New England.

There would be other side effects – economic, political, societal, and international. All of America would be affected – and much of the world – the Babylonian system would start to collapse. This would also open the door for an attack on Israel, and would likely be the start of the third world war, which we read of in Revelation.

MULTIPLE SCENARIOS

Revelation 9:17-18 "17 And thus I saw horses in the vision, and them that sat on them, having breastplates of fire, and of jacinth, and brimstone: and the heads of the horses were as the heads of lions; and out of their mouths issued fire and smoke and brimstone. 18 By these three was the third part of men killed, by the fire, by the smoke, and by the brimstone, which issued out of their mouths."

These verses are talking about one third of the people on earth being killed. I believe these verses are connected with the number 8,640. One third of the earth's population would be about 2.33 billion people. This is an enormous number. This is not just military personnel. This amount of people would mean that a great many civilians are killed as a result of this event.

What kind of event could cause this many civilians to be killed? Well, we know it is going to involve fire, smoke and brimstone. So, what events could that be?

The first and most likely is a nuclear exchange. When the United States dropped the nuclear bombs on Japan that was it – Japan surrendered. But, today that is unlikely. Today, if one country were to use a nuclear weapon on another it would lead to retaliation, either from the country under attack or their allies. This could easily escalate into a nuclear free for all.

I believe this is the scenario that will lead to the destruction of Mystery Babylon. Maybe it is the opening scene in this nuclear exchange or just part of it. While the exact details of how everything happens is unknown, we do know the end result and we do know where we are now and we know how world events are shaping up.

The table for these Revelation events is being set right now.

Certain geographical areas have great importance in terms of Biblical end time prophecy. We can look at the geometry of importance as a series of concentric circles – like a bullseye target with the center being the most important and the outer circles less important.

At the very center is the temple or temple site, then the next circle is Jerusalem, then Israel, then the Middle Eastern countries that border Israel, then the rest of the Middle East region, then on the outer circles the rest of the world.

But, understand that the entire world will be involved and feel the effects of the end time events. Some places more than others and some places less than others.

It is very important to keep a close eye on the Middle East and the nuclear talks with Iran. These events that are taking place are setting the table for the Revelation events including verses 9:17-18.

Regardless of how this all plays out, the destruction of Mystery Babylon will be a significant part of it.

Imagine Iran or terrorists get some nuclear weapons and use them to hit Israel and New York. Think about the next actions and how easily it could lead to many nuclear exchanges.

Or imagine Israel and/or other Middle Eastern Countries decide they have to hit Iran with a nuclear weapon as a preemptive measure – then Iran or its allies respond with a nuclear attack – again it is easy to see how this could lead to a great exchange of nuclear weapons being used.

This kind of scenario is what I believe will cause the destruction of Mystery Babylon – and other end time Revelation events.

However, another possibility is a natural event – most likely an asteroid strike. Though less likely, God has used natural events in the past – the destruction of Sodom and Gomorrah, and Noah's flood to name two such events.

The description of fire, smoke and brimstone could be related to a major asteroid impact.

In any case, the scriptures tell us that Mystery Babylon will fall dramatically, suddenly – in an hour, unexpectedly and the world will see it.

A nuclear event or an asteroid hit are the first and second ways this could happen.

BEYOND 2016

Jesus, tells us about the fig tree generation.

Matthew 24:32-35 KJV: "Now learn a parable of the fig tree; When his branch is yet tender, and putteth forth leaves, ye know that summer is nigh: So likewise ye, when ye shall see all these things, know that it is near, even at the doors.

Verily I say unto you, This generation shall not pass, till all these things be fulfilled.

Heaven and earth shall pass away, but my words shall not pass away."

'All these things' refers to the things Jesus mentions right before this in Matthew 24:4-31.

'It is near, even at the doors', refers to the end of the age being near, or the beginning of the end – the tribulation and soon after that the return of Jesus, the rapture and the new beginning, the new heaven and new earth.

'The fig tree', refers to the reforming of Israel as a nation. (trees generally refer to nations – sometimes people)

'This generation shall not pass, till all these things be fulfilled', refers to the length of time from the formation of Israel as a nation until all the events of Matthew 24:4-31 take place.

I believe a generation is most likely 72 years. And I believe Jesus was telling us these things would take place within that time (of a generation or within 72 years).

Of course 70 is also super important – it is 7*10

70 = 7*10. This is ten shemitah periods. 10 – the number of heaven or God's Kingdom times 7 – the number of perfection, completion, totality.

Israel became a nation in 1948 (May – the spring – the time to sow).

2018-1948=70 (70*360=25,200) a massive shemitah length of time.

2,520*10=25,200

1948+70=2018.

The year 1948 plus 10 shemitahs equals 2018

Earlier it was mentioned that in 1990 the spring equinox line entered the constellation Aquarius after spending 2,160 years in the constellation Pisces (from 170 BC to 1990 AD).

2018-1990=28 (this is 4 shemitah periods) or 4*7=28

28*360=10,080 (a great earth time number)

We could also express this as: 4 (number of earth)*2,520 (shemitah period) =10,080 or

The year 1990 plus 10,080 equals 2018.

What we are seeing is a convergence of shemitahs. One super giant shemitah ending in 2016, plus the Jerusalem shemitah in 2016 (2016-1967=49) and the Abrahamic generational shemitah, the last week of Daniels 70 weeks plus the connection with all the earth time numbers, and then another big shemitah from the formation of Israel in 1948 (2018-1948=70)=(10*7) ending in 2018, which is also 4 shemitahs from 1990.

Israel was formed in the spring (the time to sow or plant).

The fall is the time to reap or harvest. And the end of the age is the harvest time.

Daniel speaks of the 3.5 years (a time, times and half a time) (Daniel 12) in connection with the end of days and right before the return of Christ and the rapture.

If we add three and a half years to the spring of 2015 when the spring equinox occurs, we are in the fall of 2018.

The spring of 2015(March 20) was the 25th time the spring equinox line was in the constellation Aquarius. (As noted before 2015-1990=25) and (25*360=9,000) 9,000 represents entering the final hour.

If 9,000 is the beginning of the final hour what should be the end of the final hour?

At first we may think 10,000. But, I think 10,080 is more likely.

Let's calculate both.

March 20, 2015 = 9,000.

10,000-9,000 = 1,000

1,000/360=2.7777

March 20, 2015 plus 2 years equals March 20, 2017

(.7777 * 360 = 280 rounded)

280 added to March 20, 2017 equals December 25, 2017.

So, if 10,000 represents the end of the final hour it would be at the end of 2017 (December 25, 2017) which is a very interesting date.

This is obviously a possibility.

But, is it accurate? – Probably not in terms of being the end of the final hour, it is likely another sign to us marking the last of the last days.

If we use 10,080 we get a different date. 10,080-9,000=1,080.

1,080/360=3.

So, March 20, 2015 plus 3 equals March 20, 2018. (The Spring Equinox)

But, Daniel speaks of three and a half years.

If we add a half year we get (360/2=180), 180=half a year,

Therefore 1,080+180=1,260 (as in the prophecies of Daniel)

March 20, 2015 plus 3 = March 20, 2018 plus 180=September 16, 2018.

Using 10,080 as the end of the final hour puts us in the fall of 2018. The fall is harvest time, and harvest time is the end of the age.

This confirms all the dates and numbers we have examined.

Now, does this mean September 16, 2018 is the day when our Lord and Savior Jesus is going to return and the rapture will happen on that day?

No, I don't think we can be that accurate for a number of reasons, the main one being that we are using two calendars – so how do we compensate for dates? I don't think it's possible to do so accurately.

And there are other issues such as the fall equinox happens on September 22, not the 16th.

In addition we have to consider the Jewish Festival dates that year.

And on top of that we have the two hemispheres (Northern and Southern) in which the equinoxes are reversed.

I believe this is why Jesus says, of that day and hour, no man knows except the Father.

This is telling us that while we can know the season, we can't accurately calculate the exact time or day.

But, when Jesus tells us that only the Father knows the day and hour, he is saying that at moment, as Jesus is speaking, the Father already knows the day and hour.

That means that at the time Jesus is speaking the date is already set.

Just as the birth, death, resurrection and ascension of Jesus were fixed, set points in time; and just as the fall of ancient Babylon and the fall of Mystery Babylon are set, fixed points in time, so is the day and hour of the return of Jesus Christ– and it is very soon.

To be clear we are not suggesting exact dates, but rather recognizing the seasons.

From all of this we can clearly see that we are entering the final season.

THE SUM OF THE MATTERS

As Daniel said, here is the sum of the matters.

Spring 2015 marks the beginning of the final hour. In 2016 Mystery Babylon falls; causing the collapse of the entire Babylonian system, which is the end of man's system and the beginning of the end of the reign of man.

This time period from September/October 2015 to September/ October 2016 is when Mystery Babylon falls and puts us right at the beginning of the tribulation period. This is the beginning of the last week of years as per Daniel's prophecy.

The (pre-wrath) tribulation period continues for three and half years to the fall of 2018. Sometime in the fall of 2018 is when I believe we will see the return of Jesus Christ and the end of time as we know it – the return of Jesus Christ will also be the time of the rapture.

All the math and heavenly signs confirm this and match up with His word in the Holy Bible.

Look at this.

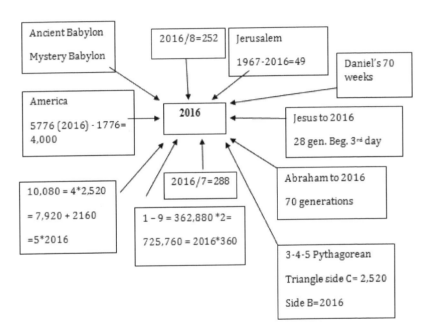

All of these things point to 2016 and they all fit together perfectly. And there is more which is not in the above diagram.

Are all of these things a coincidence?

If not, then it is by design – by God – what is He telling us?

2016 will be a year like no other. 2016 will be a gigantic year in God's end time plan.

I believe 2016 will be the most eventful year since Jesus Christ walked the earth.

We are in the very last of the last days. The last week of 7 years is about to begin.

A LAST THOUGHT ON ALL OF THIS

Some people may say this all seems too soon. Or they may say the idea of New York City (Mystery Babylon) falling in 2016 is farfetched. To this, I agree. It seems very soon to me – too soon, and the idea of New York City being destroyed is unimaginable – in the natural.

But, what we are talking about is bible prophecy. Prophetic events always seem outrageous and improbable.

In early September 2001 the idea that the twin towers would fall because of being hit by hijacked planes also seemed farfetched – until it happened. This is always the case when some earth shaking event happens – it seems impossible until it happens.

Mystery Babylon falling in 2016 seems improbable – farfetched. But, all the signs and numbers, and prophetic clues point to it.

Ultimately, what we are left with is this – Are all the things, all the numbers, all the math, all the astronomy, all the Biblical clues and everything a coincidence or do they mean something?

It is a lot to be a coincidence – too much, in my opinion.

So, it must mean something – that 2016 is the year. This is the only conclusion I can come to.

What if nothing happens in 2016? Of course God can do whatever He wants, when He wants so in that regards anything is possible. But, I believe it is unlikely nothing will happen. God has plans and a purpose, He knows the end from the beginning and has written the end and He is orchestrating and arranging events to fulfill His plan – biblical prophecy. God operates according to patterns with major events happening on predetermined appointed dates.

I believe everything discussed here reveals a part of His plan. And these things will happen according to His schedule, and that is what all the information in this book points to. I believe God showed me this and led me in this for a reason, because time is late and people need to know.

If nothing happens in 2016 – then obviously I have misinterpreted what God is saying. I absolutely believe the information here is accurate and from the LORD. I believe I have interpreted it correctly. If nothing happens in 2016 then I still will believe the information is good, but my interpretation of what it means is off. I don't think that's the case – time will tell.

8 - THE STARS PROCLAIM HIS GLORY

As noted before, in 1990 the spring equinox line entered the constellation Aquarius. It had been in Pisces since 170 BC.

Aquarius is historically known for two things.

The first, it is the water-bearer.

The second, it is the age of enlightenment.

Aquarius is the constellation representing the water bearer. Jesus Christ is the eternal water bearer.

"'You and Aaron must take the staff and assemble the entire community. As the people watch, command the rock over there to pour out its water. You will get enough water from the rock to satisfy all the people and their livestock.' So, Moses did as he was told. He took the staff from the place where it was kept before the LORD. Then he and Aaron summoned the people to come, and gather at the rock. 'Listen, you rebels!' he shouted. 'Must we bring you water from this rock?' Then, Moses raised his hand and struck the rock twice with the staff, and water gushed out. So all the people and their livestock drank their fill." (Num. 20:8-11 Tyndale NLT)

The rock here is a picture of Jesus Christ.

"I don't want you to forget, dear brothers and sisters, what happened to our ancestors in the wilderness long ago. God guided all of them by sending a cloud that moved along ahead of them, and he brought them all safely through the waters of the sea on dry ground. As followers of Moses, they were all baptized in the cloud and the sea. And all of them ate the same miraculous food, and all of them drank the same miraculous water. For they

---

all drank from the miraculous rock that traveled with them, and that rock was Christ." (1 Cor. 10: 1-4 Tyndale NLT)

And there is the event at the well with Jesus Christ and the Samaritan woman.

"Jesus answered and said unto her, 'Whosoever drinketh of this water shall thirst again: But whosoever drinketh of the water that I shall give him shall never thirst; but the water that I shall give him shall be in him a well of water springing up into everlasting life". (John 4:13-14 KJV)

So, the spring equinox line moving into the constellation Aquarius is a heavenly sign of the great coming our Lord Jesus Christ. It signals His return. It is written in the stars – Jesus Christ will return while the equinox line is in Aquarius – He is the water-bearer.

Aquarius is also known as the age of enlightenment. The age of enlightenment is a period of increased knowledge. Daniel ties this to the end of the age.

"But thou, O Daniel, shut up the words, and seal the book, even to the time of the end: many shall run to and fro, and knowledge shall be increased". (Dan. 12:4 KJV)

This verse is linking the increase in knowledge to the end times. The equinox line moving into the constellation Aquarius in 1990 begins this time of increased knowledge – which also connects it to the end of the age.

Technology exploded right around 1990, from a couple of years before to a few years after. It was during this time we saw the computer become a common household item, the creation of the world wide web, and the invention of the smart phone – all in the years right around 1990, when the equinox line entered Aquarius.

This is confirmation of the verse from Daniel. We have entered the final countdown – and March 20, 2015 marks the 25th time the equinox line appears in Aquarius. 25*360=9,000, which is the beginning of the final hour.

What we see is a lining up of the stars as God's messengers and scripture – both coming together telling us the same thing, and telling us the time is now.

THE LION AND THE SICKLE

THE HEART OF THE LION IS TO USE THE SICKLE

There are two yearly equinoxes – spring and fall. The spring is on March 20 and the fall on September 22 in the Northern Hemisphere. In the southern Hemisphere it is reversed – the Spring equinox is September 22 and the Fall equinox is March 20.

We will use the Northern Hemisphere as that is where most readers will be. It is also where the United States of America and Israel are located.

In 1990, a 2,160 year period ended and the equinox line moved into new constellations after being in the previous constellations since 170 BC.

The equinox line is a line drawn from earth looking due east at sunrise on the equinox dates – so we would see the sun rise in a particular constellation year after year for 2,160 years. It takes that long for the equinox line to move through each constellation.

The spring equinox line (Northern Hemisphere) entered the constellation Aquarius on March 20, 1990.

The Fall equinox line also moved into a new constellation on September 22, 1990 (Northern Hemisphere). And September 22, 2015 will be the 25th time the equinox line will be in this new constellation. So, the math is the same – it marks the 9th hour.

The Spring Equinox marks seed time, the time to sow, or to plant.

The Fall Equinox marks harvest time, or the time reap.

The Fall Equinox line had been in Virgo since 170 BC. Virgo represents the Virgin Mary. Jesus was born while the fall equinox line was in Virgo, and all of Christianity took place during this time – until 1990.

In 1990 the Fall Equinox line entered the constellation Leo – also known as The Lion.

The first time Jesus came, He came as the Lamb, the next time Jesus comes, He comes as the Lion.

"And I saw another mighty angel come down from heaven, clothed with a cloud: and a rainbow was upon his head, and his face was as it were the sun, and his feet as pillars of fire:

And he had in his hand a little book open: and he set his right foot upon the sea, and his left foot upon the earth,

And cried with a loud voice, as when a lion roareth: and when he had cried, seven thunders uttered their voices." (Rev. 10:1-3 KJV)

Who is Jesus? He is the Lion of the tribe of Judah.

"And one of the elders saith unto me, Weep not: behold the Lion of the tribe of Juda, the Root of David, hath prevailed to open the book, and to loose the seven seals thereof." (Rev. 5:5 KJV)

The first time Jesus came, He came as the Lamb, the next time – when Jesus Christ returns, He will come as the Lion.

When is the end of the age? The end of the age is harvest time.

"The enemy that sowed them is the devil: the harvest is the end of the world; and the reapers are the angels." (Matt. 13:39 KJV)

How does one harvest or reap? He uses a sickle to harvest or reap.

"But when the fruit is brought forth, immediately he putteth in the sickle, because the harvest is come." (Mark 4:29 KJV)

We see the heavens declaring the word of God – lining up with scripture, confirming it, proclaiming it – telling us the season we are in.

The constellation Leo (the Lion) is notable for a couple of reasons.

Within the constellation Leo the Lion is a group of six stars, known as the sickle.

This group starts with the main star Regulus, which is located in the heart of the Lion.

Regulus does double duty, it is also the first star at the end of the handle of the sickle. The sickle then curves up the neck and mane area of Leo, and then curves again tightly above the head.

Regulus is the heart of the Lion and the first part of the handle of the sickle. The heart represents the will and intention of the Lion (Jesus Christ). The handle is where one puts their hand to use the sickle.

In other words the heart of the Lion is to use the sickle – the heart of our Lord and Savior Jesus is to use the sickle - to reap the harvest.

In September 1990, the Fall Equinox line entered Leo.

The sickle appears in the constellation Leo the Lion as a smaller group of six stars.

The word 'sickle' appears in the (KJV) Bible 12 times.

12 means divine rule, or divine government.

Of the 12 times the word 'sickle' appears in the Bible, 7 are in the book of Revelation. Revelation - being the main prophetic end time book. The number 7 means completeness, totality, perfection.

And all 7 occurrences of the word 'sickle' in Revelation are in chapter 14.

The Autumn Equinox of 2015 on September 22, marks the beginning of the final hour as it pertains to the harvest. (9 equals finality, the 9th hour is the final hour)

The equinox line entered Leo September 22, 1990. 2015-1990=25 years.

25*360=9,000.

Revelation chapter 14 tells of the reaping. In this we see a summary of end times events and then we see Jesus Christ using the sickle to gather (reap/harvest) the saints and we see a (another) angel of heaven use the sickle to gather (reap/harvest) those who have rejected the LORD and bring them to the winepress of God's wrath.

Here is Revelation 14 (KJV) with the word 'sickle' bolded by the author.

Revelation 14:

"1 And I looked, and, lo, a Lamb stood on the mount Si'-on, and with him an hundred forty and four thousand, having his Father's name written in their foreheads.

2 And I heard a voice from heaven, as the voice of many waters, and as the voice of a great thunder: and I heard the voice of harpers harping with their harps:

3 And they sung as it were a new song before the throne, and before the four beasts, and the elders: and no man could learn that song but the hundred and forty and four thousand, which were redeemed from earth.

4 These are they which were not defiled with women; for they are virgins. These are they which follow the Lamb whithersoever he goeth. These were redeemed from among men, being the firstfruits unto God and the Lamb.

5 And in their mouth was found no guile: for they are without fault before the throne of God.

6 And I saw another angel fly in the midst of heaven, having the everlasting gospel to preach unto them that dwell on the earth, and to every nation, and kindred, and tongue, and people.

7 Saying with a loud voice, Fear God, and give glory to him; for the hour of his judgment is come: and worship him that made heaven, and earth, and the sea, and the fountains of waters.

8 And there followed another angel, saying, Babylon, is fallen, is fallen, that great city, because she made all nations drink of the wine of the wrath of her fornication.

9 And the third angel followed them, saying with a loud voice, If any man worship the beast, and his image, and receive his mark in his forehead, or in his hand,

10 The same shall drink of the wine of the wrath of God, which is poured out without mixture into the cup of his indignation; and he shall be tormented with fire and brimstone in the presence of the holy angels, and in the presence of the Lamb:

11 And the smoke of their torment ascendeth up for ever and ever: and they have no rest day nor night, who worship the beast and his image, and whosoever receiveth the mark of his name.

12 Here is the patience of the saints: here are they that keep the commandments of God, and the faith of Jesus.

13 And I heard a voice from heaven saying unto me, Write, Blessed are the dead which die in the Lord from henceforth: Yea, saith the Spirit, that they may rest from their labours; and their works do follow them.

14 And I looked, and behold a white cloud, and upon the cloud one sat like unto the Son of man, having on his head a golden crown, and **in his hand a sharp sickle.**

15 And another angel came out of the temple, crying with a loud voice to him that sat on the cloud, **Thrust in thy sickle** and reap: for the time is come for thee to reap; for the harvest of the earth is ripe.

16 And he that sat on the cloud **thrust in his sickle** on the earth; and the earth was reaped.

17 And another angel came out of the temple which is in heaven, **he also having a sharp sickle.**

18 And another angel came from the alter, which had power over fire; and cried with a loud cry to him **that had the sharp sickle**, saying, **Thrust in thy sharp sickle**, and gather the clusters of the vine of the earth; for her grapes are fully ripe.

19 And the angel **thrust in his sickle** into the earth, and gathered the vine of the earth, and cast it into the great winepress of the wrath of God.

20 And the winepress was trodden without the city, and blood came out of the winepress, even unto the horse bridles, by the space of a thousand and six hundred furlongs."

It is interesting that there are six stars in the sickle in the constellation Leo, and the word sickle appears 7 times in six verses here in Revelation.

The Fall Equinox line is now in the constellation Leo the Lion where the sickle is located, where the heart of the Lion is to put his hand on the sickle, and to use it to gather his saints, this shows us the time when all of these things shall be fulfilled is near.

Halleluiah!

The Stars Declare His Glory

"The heavens declare the glory of God; and the firmament showeth His handywork.

Day unto day uttereth speech, and night unto night showeth knowledge.

There is no speech nor language, where their voice is not heard.

Their line is gone out through all the earth, and their words to the end of the world. In them hath he set a tabernacle for the sun,

Which is as a bridegroom coming out of his chamber, and rejoiceth as a strong man to run a race.

His going forth is from the end of the heaven, and his circuit unto the ends of it: and there is nothing hid from the heat thereof". (Ps. 19:1-6 KJV)

The stars are messengers of God, declaring His word to everyone, every tribe, nation and people.

Let us understand what He is telling us through them.

9 - WHAT'S IN A NUMBER

The information in this section is given to show the numbers used in the calculations are valid. Just in case you are sharing this with someone who challenges you on the accuracy of the numbers, and they say the numbers aren't accurate.

The numbers used are actually very accurate – not 100%, but this small difference is irrelevant.

I'm speaking specifically about three numbers, 7,920 as the diameter of the earth in miles, 2,160 as the number of years it takes for the equinox line to move through a constellation and 72 years as the number of years it takes for the equinox line to move 1 degree.

The numbers used here are those historically used. These are the numbers used in stories and myths from around the world throughout time. This was the way knowledge was passed down in the past.

As a fictional example - a story may say something like this: There is a group of 30 apple trees with 72 apples on each making up 1 orchard and there are a total of 12 orchards.

In this type of story we can see all the relevant numbers – and those who understand how to calculate would know this is really about time and the constellations. They would recognize this as a way of communicating important information. From this they would know the number of major constellations, the time for the equinox line to move through each, the time for the equinox line to move 1 degree and the time for a full cycle through all 12.

We can easily see how it is necessary to use whole numbers in a story like this. You can have 72 apples, but not 71.6 – the story wouldn't make sense.

Daniel would have been familiar with many of these myths and stories. I absolutely believe Daniel would have done his calculations the way we did, using the numbers we did. And remember, Daniel received his knowledge from God. (Dan. 1:17). Therefore, I believe this is the way God wants us to do the calculations.

Today we have more technology and can calculate more accurately, but it doesn't matter because the differences are so small.

For example, according to about.com geography on 2/27/15 the diameter of the earth at the equator is 7,926.41 miles. We used 7,920. The difference is a mere 6.41 miles. 6.41/7926.41=.0008086 or .08 percent. So, our number 7,920 is over 99.9% accurate. The difference is insignificant, it is a rounding error – so small it doesn't matter.

According to Graham Hancock's book 'Finger-Prints of the Gods', the actual modern day calculation of time it takes for the equinox line to move through a constellation is 2,148 years or 71.6 years to move 1 degree (71.6*30 degrees = 2,148).

The difference is minuscule. .4/71.6 = .0055865 or .55865 percent. Our number of 72 years is over 99% accurate – like wise our number of 2,160 years.

The difference doesn't matter because it so small.

Keep in mind how we calculate our calendar. We use a 365 day calendar based on how long it takes the earth to complete a full circuit around the sun. But, our calendar isn't 100% accurate. According to answers.com science on 2/27/15 it takes 365.2425 days. We adjust our calendar every four years with a leap year by adding a day – and this is still not 100% accurate.

Would we say that since our calendar is off about .25 days per year it doesn't work? Do we consider our calendar useless or meaningless? No, we know it is off a small amount and we make an adjustment and it works. Anyway, how would you have a fraction of a day?

The amount it is off is .2425/365 = .0006643 or .06643 percent. So, it is also over 99.9% accurate.

Our numbers and calculations regarding the diameter of the earth and the time for the equinox line to travel through the constellations are all in the same accuracy range – all over 99%.

Bottom line, the small difference is irrelevant and doesn't matter. We are using the numbers Daniel would have almost certainly used, and they are actually quite accurate.

Another note on this topic – the 12 main constellations are not all the same size, so the time it takes for the equinox line to move through a particular constellation may vary a little. This too is irrelevant.

Although they are different sizes, they are fairly evenly spaced – it's convenient how it's designed this way. So, the time it takes for the equinox line to move through each constellation can be determined to be the same.

It is a calculation based on convenience. 12 constellations fairly evenly spaced simply equally divided. 360 degrees in a sphere divided by 12 gives us 30 degrees for each constellation, and 2,160/30=72 years for 1 degree. So, much like the other numbers and our calendar, it is accurate to a fairly high degree. In short, it works. The fact that they are not all the same size is irrelevant.

And lastly the 360 days in a Biblical year is consistent. Although most cultures switched to a 365 day solar calendar prior 539 BC it doesn't matter. Throughout the Bible a year is considered to be 360 days. So, in our math this is what we need to use in relation to Biblical prophecy and God's great earth time clock.

We have 2 calendars so we need to adjust and compensate where relevant – as we did measuring from the fall of Ancient Babylon to Mystery Babylon. Of course God knew we would have two calendars so the difference can be reconciled as it is in our calculations.

Again, this information is just so you will know the accuracy in case you are sharing with someone and they question the accuracy of the numbers etc.

The bottom line is that it all works and is actually very accurate.

10 - THIS IS THE TIME

I am very concerned that many people who think they are going to be with the LORD forever will not be. Throughout the entire bible the pattern is always the same – 50% are accepted and 50% are not.

And this is not referring to the world at large. Among the world at large only a remnant is truly saved. It is always a remnant of God's people that survives.

Starting with Abel and Cain we see the pattern of 50% of those who say they belong to God being accepted and 50% rejected. Both Abel and Cain declared to be followers of God by the fact they each brought an offering. So, both proclaimed to be followers of God; Abel was accepted and Cain rejected. 50%.

In the New Testament we read of two being in the field and one chosen, and one left. We also read of the ten bridesmaids, five get to go to the wedding and five don't. It is always 50%. Why? Because that is exactly what it will be – 50% - of those who claim to be followers of Jesus Christ.

Some people may say that this represents the Jews or the world at large, but that's not the case. Jesus was speaking to his followers when he told us this.

Bridesmaids are those who expect to go to a wedding – this represents those who say they believe in Jesus as their Savior – those who believe they will go to the wedding in heaven.

So, it is time to fully commit to the LORD. It is time to put God first. It is time for the church to get real – to stop playing church and time to be the church as God intended.

It is time to wake up. It is time to focus on doing God's will and His work.

THE CHURCH

Jesus didn't preach about the church – He preached about the Kingdom.

"From that time Jesus began to preach, and say, 'Repent: for the Kingdom of heaven is at hand.'" (Matt. 4:17 KJV)

In the four gospels He only mentions the word church three times.

But, today we see the church preaching all about the church. The church loves to talk about the church.

They should be preaching about how great Jesus Christ our LORD and Savior is, and His Kingdom.

The church in general is failing, because they are asleep and don't recognize the season we are in.

In Revelation chapters 2 and 3 we see what Jesus has to say about the church. Much of it is not good.

Jesus is not coming for the church – He is coming for the saints, the remnant.

The church is sound asleep and needs to wake up.

After 9/11 people flocked to the church – it looked like a real revival would take place in America. People were truly moved, their hearts were honestly touched and they came in truth to church in droves seeking truth, seeking answers. But, the church wasn't ready. The church didn't have any answers. The church was clueless and oblivious.

The people realized this and stopped going; and the revival that could have been wasn't. People came seeking truth and answers and didn't get either because the church was sound asleep. The sad fact is that here we are now 14 years later and most of the church is still sound asleep. Most of the church is oblivious about the season we are in, and they are still preaching all about the church – not about Jesus Christ and the Kingdom of heaven – so they are leading many astray.

Christians are supposed to be the light and show other people the way.

Today it is very hard to tell the difference between someone who claims to be a Christian from the rest of the world. The church suffers from everything the rest of the world suffers from. In some cases people who claim to be Christians are worse than the rest of the world. These days it's hard to tell what's important to the church. What does the church stand for? What is the church willing to fight for?

As mentioned before my main ministry is to help bring animal lovers and Christians together and to teach what God's word says regarding His lesser creatures, because most Christians are clueless in this area.

The church shouldn't be clueless – or missing in action. There are a lot of terrible abuses to animals happening all over today – and the church is completely silent. It's a very strange version of church that exists today.

The church and Christians are supposed to be leading the way, speaking out against evil, speaking for righteousness, and leading by example.

 But, for the most part the church is silent – having very little impact on the world – losing influence, because they have a lukewarm religious attitude and not a true heart for the Lord. The world, (meaning most people), see this weakness and recognize the phoniness, hypocrisy and lack of truth, and turn away.

The people are crying out for truth and are seeking wisdom and understanding. They are, in their spirit, desperate to know the LORD, but they don't recognize it is the LORD they are seeking because of the false impression of Christianity that is prevalent in the church today – so they leave – and the for the most part the church remains silent about important matters, clueless, irrelevant and asleep; and no different than the rest of the world.

America is in trouble, and in the next few years will go through a radical transformation.

The reason America is in trouble and going the wrong way is not because of the people and it is not because of our political leaders.

It is because of the weak and ineffective church. The church is focused almost solely on the church.

There used to be an expression, "It's all about me." And we all have heard about the "me generation." This displays a very self centered, self focused, selfish mindset. Much of the church today is still in this mode. It is all about – how can I get blessed, how can I receive more, How can I. Self centered instead of Christ centered. Obsessed with self will and ignoring God's will.

If the church and Christians were being who they are supposed to be, their influence would be the main influence in our nation. Political leaders would be looking to the church and many political leaders would in fact come from the church – the church would be the greatest source of policy and decision making in America and America would be blessed, more united, stronger, and the light to the world - as it is supposed to be.

It is time to be who the LORD called us to be, for real, 100% - it is time to seek His will and do His will – not ours. It is time to put the LORD and His will first, honestly, truthfully without any falseness. It is time to follow Christ and not the world. It is time to follow the spirit and not the flesh. It is time to be the light we are called to be. It is time for the church to wake up.

"36 Master, which is the greatest commandment in the law?

37 Jesus said unto him, 'THOU SHALT LOVE THE LORD THY GOD WITH ALL THY HEART, AND WITH ALL THY SOUL, AND WITH ALL THY MIND.

38 This is the first and great commandment." (Matt. 22: 36-38 KJV)

The church is asleep. The church doesn't recognize the season – the church is out of season. There is a disconnect between the season we are in and the message the church is giving. Their message is becoming increasingly irrelevant.

It's like a gardening show that talks about planting tomatoes in the middle of winter – or protecting your plants from freezing in the middle of summer.

If you plant a tomato seed in the ground outside in the middle of winter – it dies, because it is out of season. The church is out of season.

The church is oblivious to the season we are in today and they are still preaching last season's message. It is a message out of time – out of step with time.

There is a principle about the relevance and value of information. Information is only valuable if it is correct and it is timely. Having good information at the wrong time is useless and pointless. What good are better driving directions after you have completed your trip?

The church has lost influence because they don't understand the time we are in. The church is sound asleep and needs to wake up. They are on the verge of being completely dead – it is time to awaken and strengthen what little remains – the time is late.

Message to the church: WAKE UP! Now is the time to seek the Lord with all your heart, soul and mind – be who you are called by the LORD to be. Do what the LORD has called you to do.

11 - CONCLUSION

Some people may look at all of this as doom and gloom – they may even get fearful.

But God's word continually tells us not to fear, but to have faith. Fear is a lack of faith. We are to be faithful not fearful.

To those of us who belong to the Lord this is not a time of doom and gloom. This is a time to rejoice – even if we have to endure some hardship because all of this points to the return of Christ our Savior and His perfect eternal kingdom.

To those who have not accepted Jesus Christ as their Lord and Savior – then yes, you should be fearful.

If you have not accepted Jesus as your Lord and Savior, then now is the time.

If you would like to accept Jesus Christ as your personal LORD and SAVIOR then say the following prayer out loud and from the heart:

"Dear Father in Heaven, I come to you in the name of Jesus Christ, I confess that I am a sinner and have sinned against you. I am sorry for sinning against you and living outside of your will, and I ask here and now for your forgiveness in the name of Jesus Christ.

I accept your only begotten son Jesus as my LORD and SAVIOR, and I believe with all my heart that Jesus died for my sins, paying my sin debt in full, and that you raised him from the dead, giving me eternal life through Jesus Christ.

Thank you Father, for forgiving my sins and I believe that as of this moment I am a new creation, born again and eternally saved. May you lead me and guide me so that I may bring glory and honor to your name.

Thank you also, Jesus Christ my LORD and SAVIOR, for dying for me and giving me eternal life.

Amen."

If you have just accepted Jesus Christ as your LORD and SAVIOR congratulations!

Halleluiah!

You may wonder what's next.

My suggestion is this – get two versions of the Bible and start by reading Genesis and then the New Testament – then go back to the rest of the Bible. The Bibles I recommend are the King James Version and the Tyndale New Living Translation (NLT) – make sure it is a Tyndale as some NLT versions are lacking spiritually.

Also, pray every day – ask God to lead you and guide you to Him – ask for understanding – just converse with Him truthfully – and ask Him to speak to you in a way you will understand – He will.

Limit the ungodly stuff you take in – news, entertainment etc. and find some good teachers who can help you grow in understanding and in Christ. Here are some of the one's I recommend on TV.

Charles Stanley – 'In Touch Ministries'

Andrew Wommack – 'The Gospel Truth'

Joseph Prince – 'Destined To Reign'

T.D. Jakes – 'The Potter's Touch'

Jim Bakker – 'The Jim Bakker Show'

Joyce Meyer – 'Enjoying Everyday Life'

I don't agree 100% with any of them – but I do mostly agree with their teaching and interpretation – I believe for the most part they are teaching the word of God correctly and are spiritually alive.

I recommend waiting to find a church. These days there are too many unbiblical or spiritually dead churches. A good church can be a great blessing, but a bad church can be damaging to your faith and Christian walk. It takes a spirit of discernment and Biblical understanding to tell a good church from a bad one.

Ask the Lord and He will tell you when to look for a church. The most important things you should consider when looking for in a church are: Do they teach biblical truth? And, is it spiritually alive? – Is it filled with the spirit of Christ?

Unfortunately, these two things are hard to find – just make sure you can recognize them when present and know when they are lacking.

God Bless You,

Henry Rhyne

ADDITIONAL INFORMATION

As I was putting the final touches on this book a couple of news stories caught my eye.

The first was that on March 20, 2015 a late winter storm hit the Northeast. This was after an unusually harsh winter. I believe this late winter storm hitting on the day of the spring (vernal) equinox was a prophetic event. I believe it is a warning of something greater to come to this area. The boundary of the snowfall of this storm started at Washington, DC – our nation's capital - and it continued northward to and through New York City.

Exactly one week later (7 days) on March 27, 2015 there was a major power outage in Amsterdam, Europe. Amsterdam – loosely meaning 'land on many waters' as in the description of Mystery Babylon in Revelation. And of course, New York City was called New Amsterdam before it was called New York. Could this also be a warning regarding Mystery Babylon? I believe it is.

Another prophetic event happened on April 7, 2015. The day before on April 6, president Obama gave a speech trying to sell the Iran nuke deal. Then the next day, on April 7, Washington, DC (our nation's capital) had a major power outage. This is a warning for us not to line up with Iran against Israel.

That's 2 major power outages in this short time – both to important cities – Amsterdam and Washington, DC.

There are three cities that have a bull statue. All three are major financial centers and all three have in their names a reference to the phrase 'land upon many waters' as we see in the book of Revelation as the location of Mystery Babylon.

The three cities are: New York City (New Amsterdam), Amsterdam, and Shanghai, China. These three represent the world wide Babylonian system – the system that is all over the world.

They also represent, old world (Amsterdam), recent/present (New Amsterdam) and New/Future (Shanghai). We could say these three represent the past, present and future Babylonian system.

When Mystery Babylon falls and the system collapses, all three of these cities will suffer greatly.

Keep an eye on all three of these cities. Whenever something happens in any of them it could very well be a prophetic event related to the fall of Mystery Babylon.

As Jonathan Cahn notes in his book "The Harbinger", the destruction of the twin towers on 9-11-2001 was a prophetic warning from God to our nation. It was a replaying of events that took place in ancient Israel. It was a warning that we had turned away from God and needed to turn back.

But, we didn't turn back to God – instead our rebellion toward God has only increased. We didn't rebuild in the name of God but in defiance of almighty God – just as ancient Israel did. After ancient Israel did this judgment came in the form of destruction. The new tower – the One World Center is the embodiment of our nation's rebellion toward God. The new tower represents the rebellion.

First there is a warning – a nation can either repent and God will heal the land or rebel and God will exact judgment and bring destruction to the land. We have rebelled instead of repenting.

So, how long is it until the judgment comes? Most people try to figure out the number years from the warning or beginning of the rebellion until the judgment. But, this is the wrong way to look at it. The number of years are irrelevant. The biblical pattern is this: if the warning is not heeded, then the actual act of rebellion begins – this is different than simply turning away from God – it is turning against Him – opposed to Him.

God's heart is always for mercy so He will delay judgment until the act of rebellion is complete – giving people a chance to repent. But, once the act of rebellion is complete then there is no chance for mercy – judgment will come.

If the new tower represents our rebellion – then the beginning of its construction (or planning) represented the beginning of our rebellion toward God. And the completion or opening of the tower would therefore represent the completion of our rebellion.

May 29, 2015 the tower officially opened to the public. That same day a government economic report was released showing that first quarter GDP shrank (was negative) .7%.

Why did these two events take place on the same day? And why .7%?

I believe this is prophetic confirmation that God's judgment on our nation is close at hand and the destruction of Mystery Babylon will be the main event in that judgment.

12 – A PREVIEW OF TWO BOOKS

Special Note – parts of the following preview may be copied and shared freely as long as they are **not sold** and refer to this book as the source; with a limit of five hundred words maximum. If you wish to use more please contact me – see inside book at beginning for contact information. This only applies to this section – for all other parts of this book regular copyright laws apply. See inside front of book.

The following section contains rough draft excerpts from two upcoming books. I was working on these two books when God gave me the information in this book. I felt an urgency to get this book out, so I put the other two on brief hold while I worked on this book – "The Secret Ancient Code Of Daniel".

These two other books have to do with the subject of animals in the Bible and our role regarding God's lesser creatures. Many people mistakenly think these are unimportant subjects. But when we see what God's word says about His creatures, we gain a much greater understanding of God and His amazing plan, and we gain a greater appreciation of God himself.

It is only the vanity of man that considers this to be less important. It surprises many when they see what the living God has to say on this subject. Understanding His word in all its glory is critical in these last days.

While studying and working on these two books, I experienced the most supernatural time in my life, with lots of amazing things taking place including being healed in a single night of a very severe respiratory illness I had for 14 years.

During this time God gave me a supernatural visible confirmation that what I was writing was true according to His word. Late at night was a most unusual sky – I saw this just minutes after asking for the Lord to give me a sign of confirmation.

The sky was blanketed in clouds with not a single visible star anywhere. Then it dawned on me that it was light out – very light. I looked up again and couldn't find a single star anywhere because of the thick cloud cover – but there was a full moon and there was a perfectly formed round circle of clear sky right around the moon letting the light shine down – the moon appeared to be straight overhead at the time. There was a highlighted ring of light around the moon. It lasted for several minutes. That was the only time I ever saw a sky like that – never before and never since.

During this time one of my dogs named Phoebee passed. Three days later I released her ashes at the beach just before sunrise, and as I was praying just before releasing her ashes I physically felt an angel's hand or the Lord's hand on my shoulder as I was praying, the pressure on my shoulder was increasing as I was praying – then I heard an audible voice saying, "Let her go. Let her go." I finished praying quickly and the hand left my shoulder, then this field of energy (like electricity) swirled upward and around my head and left. And I was left standing there in awe. A few minutes later the sunrise came over the ocean horizon and it was one of the most spectacular sunrises I have ever seen. I know it was a sign from God that heaven had just received a very special soul.

Another dog of mine (Snoop) was about 10 months old and I had her about four months at this time. While playing she slipped her collar and ran off and was missing for three days. This happened while I was working on these two books also. I spent these three days looking for her and posting flyers, searching through neighborhoods, knocking on doors, going through the woods – everywhere I could think of – from before dawn to after sunset each day – praying as I was searching asking God to help me find her.

After three days of this I was completely exhausted (I was still sick then), and I basically just collapsed on the living room floor when I came home. As I lay there I heard the voice of the Lord tell me to put flyers out at businesses on a particular road. I was so tired I couldn't move. Then I heard the voice again – louder saying, "Get Up! Go put flyers at the businesses on this road".

I sprang up, made about forty more copies of flyers and went out into the dark of night and spent a few more hours putting out flyers where the Lord had told me.

I came home and fell down on the bed and went to sleep in my clothes, fully dressed.

The next morning I went out before dawn searching some more. About ten o'clock I came home and checked my messages. A woman called saying she had Snoop. It turns she had just moved to town and had a handyman doing some work on her house. Snoop showed up at her house late the previous day (the day I collapsed on the floor and heard God speak). She and the handyman decided to keep Snoop on the screened porch for the night and they would figure out what to do the next day.

The next morning the handyman was headed to her house and stopped at a convenience store for coffee and saw the flyer I had put out the night before – on the road and location where the Lord told me to place it the night before. That day I got Snoop back (she had been miles away), thanks to the Lord – and the kindness of these two people.

The way I originally got Snoop in the first place was supernatural as well. Maxi – the first dog I had on my own – died three days prior to Snoop showing up. As I was feeding Daisy and Bee (my other two dogs) the Holy Spirit compelled me to stop in my tracks – literally putting the can of food down, and leaving their bowls on the counter. I was drawn to walk out of the kitchen and through the living room and look out the front door. Just at that precise moment – that very instant, Snoop was walking right by my front door. A second earlier or later and I would have completely missed her. She was in pitiful shape, and nearly starving, every bone on her body was clearly visible.

I brought her in and fed her along with my other dogs – then she collapsed right there and slept for hours. For three days all she did was eat, sleep and go out to do her business. I tried to find her owner but never could so I kept her – I believe the way she arrived was totally of God and somehow there had been some type of spiritual communication from my dog Maxi that had passed three days earlier, and God and Snoop – as if Maxi (who was a shelter dog – most likely from a medical testing facility) had talked with God and God saw Snoop in need and deliberately sent her to me.

She was a great blessing – sadly she passed due to cancer when she was just five years old. Five as in the number of grace – as if she was sent by grace and a sign of grace. She didn't suffer long – it was quick. She was a miracle dog.

And there were other supernatural events as well that took place during the course of working on these two books. It was during this time that Jesus Christ appeared to me in a dream and gave me a vision of heaven. And there were other vision-dreams during this time.

I believe this high level of Godly supernatural activity is a sign that what I was working on was of God and very important to Him.

In fact, the revelation God gave me for this book ultimately came out my studying and prayer and revelation of the two other books concerning God's animals.

There are many deep issues connected with God's lesser creatures and these issues are related to America in the last days, and to many people who claim to be Christians. This subject ties in with prophecy, deception, the saved and unsaved, eternity, the nature of heaven and the heart of God.

It is a neglected but very important Biblical subject.

My purpose is to build a bridge between animal lovers and Christians.

My first love and passion as a Christian is to teach and share, especially regarding God's other creatures. My primary purpose is to help those who have lost animals they love find peace and comfort in God's word.

My secondary goal is to teach animal lovers what the Bible says and lead them to Christ through that.

Thirdly, is to teach Christians what the Bible says about our relationship as stewards over God's animals and how we should treat them.

This rough draft preview is from excerpts of the books on this subject. (Coming soon)

ALL ANIMALS GO TO HEAVEN

Will your pets go to heaven? Yes, absolutely.

Beyond that I absolutely believe that every animal that has ever existed since the time of Adam and Eve in the Garden of Eden will have eternal life with Christ our Lord.

Do you doubt this?

I have no doubt about this whatsoever – I am as certain of this as I am about anything. I am as certain about this as I am that 2+2=4.

This may be too big a vision for some people. Their vision of God is too small.

The God I know is huge, enormous beyond all comprehension – unlimited and almighty. God could bring every single animal that has ever existed to heaven with just one word – 'come'.

"33 O the depth of the riches both of the wisdom and knowledge of God! How unsearchable are his judgments and his ways past finding out!

34 FOR WHO HATH KNOWN THE MIND OF THE LORD? OR WHO HATH BEEN HIS COUNSELLOR?

35 OR WHO HATH FIRST GIVEN TO HIM, AND IT SHALL BE RECOMPENSED UNTO HIM AGAIN?

36 For of him and through him, and to him, are all things: to whom be the glory forever. A-men" (Rom. 11:33-36 KJV)

Before I get to Biblical evidence – let me address the arguments against this view. Basically the only reasons someone would think that all animals don't have eternal life with the LORD are either because of pride or a lack of understanding of the word.

Some people may think that by stating that animals do not go to heaven they are somehow elevating man. They are trying to raise man higher by diminishing animals. This is misguided – man is above animals – and God cares more about man than animals.

So, if God cares enough about His lesser creatures to bring them with Him for all eternity, think how much more this elevates man in God's eyes. If God will raise up His lowly animals, how much more will He raise up man.

Diminishing the importance of animals to God lowers the importance of man, and diminishes God. It doesn't make God bigger – it makes Him smaller. It doesn't give Him more glory – it takes glory from Him.

Pride is one reason people are reluctant to accept that all animals will go to heaven – and that really shows a lack of faith, a lack of trust about what God's word says about man. Pride thinks it has to add something to God's word, because God's word is insufficient.

I believe all animals go to heaven and that makes God larger, it makes heaven larger, it gives God more glory, and it increases the value and importance of man in God's plan.

Some people may deny that all animals go to heaven because of a lack of understanding of God's word. This comes down to two possible rationales that are both incorrect.

One is that God can't bring all His animals to heaven forever, meaning He lacks the power or ability.

This is obviously false. This is limiting God. God is all powerful, and there is nothing that is beyond His ability to do. If He can create the heavens and the earth and all the animals, and people, and angels, and if He is capable of giving eternal life to His saints then He certainly has the ability to give all animals eternal life. This is a piece of cake for God.

Keep in mind that animals are innocent and have never sinned. They are created by God and belong to Him. He called them good.

Second, people may say, well, God can do it, but that doesn't mean He will. In other words they say He has the ability, but chooses not to. This is also limiting God. This is saying that God doesn't love them enough, or God doesn't care enough, or God doesn't have enough mercy, or kindness.

God is love. God is merciful, God is kind, God cares for all His creatures, He calls them good, and God is just and righteous. God is all of these things and more without limit. God is infinite in love and mercy and kindness. To say that God has the ability to give all of His animals eternal life, but chooses not to, limits God in all of these areas.

Not only that, but it makes parts of God's word untrue. Think about an unwanted kitten or puppy that is killed for convenience. Think of a new born wild animal that is killed in its infancy by a predator. Think of an animal that has the misfortune of being in an animal testing facility, or a factory farm. Think of an animal that is born and only knows pain and suffering and then death.

If God just allowed such animals to be born, suffer, experience pain and die and that was it, and nothing else; how could we say God is love? How could we say God is merciful or kind, or just, or righteous?

If God would allow such animals to be born and just suffer and die and that was it – then He wouldn't be love, He wouldn't be merciful, or kind, or just or righteous. It would be very cruel.

It would be against God's nature and it would make His word untrue.

So, in this regard, God has a problem, much like He did with Abraham concerning Isaac. God will not allow any part of His word to be untrue. Nor is God's nature anything less than 100% love, 100% merciful, 100% just, 100% righteous. One thing I have learned in this study is that God will make sure that every single letter of His word is true – He will go to extraordinary lengths to keep His word, every single bit of it.

God's nature and His word demand that He gives all of His animals eternal life. Otherwise, there are huge problems and contradictions in His word.

We know that God's word and character are true, so we can know that all animals will have eternal life with the LORD. (BTW: The same is true of children who have died young – they are innocent – therefore automatically saved).

In the Garden of Eden there was no pain, suffering or death for man or animals before Adam and Eve sinned. This was God's original will and intention. God does not change – His will and intention do not change. His original will and intention then is still His will and intention now. The whole of the Bible and all of history is about the fulfilling of God's original will and intention.

The Garden of Eden is a picture of heaven and in it all created beings had eternal life.

When we read the creation account in Genesis in modern English Bibles we don't get the original meaning because the words used do not reflect the original Hebrew accurately.

In our modern English translations we see the word 'beast' or 'creature'. But in the original the word is 'living soul' or 'life' with a note in the margins saying that 'life' means 'living soul'. The original Hebrew words are 'nephesh' or 'nephesh chayah', which means living soul.

All life comes from God – man and animals both have the same creator, both come from dust, both have the same breath – the breath of God – which imparts a living soul. All life comes from God – all life is sacred and eternal, because our creator is sacred and eternal.

In his book, 'The Immortality Of Animals And The Relation Of Man As Guardian, From A Biblical And Philosophical Hypothesis', E.D. Buckner M.D. writes that he checked older versions of the Bible and stopped checking when he found 100 versions of older Bibles that used the term 'living souls' to refer to animals in the creation account or the term 'life' with a note in the margin saying that 'life' means 'living soul'.

The Darby translation most closely reflects the original language and meaning of the creation account – here is part of that account.

"19 And there was evening, and there was morning – a fourth day.

20 And God said, Let the waters swarm with swarms of living souls, and let fowl fly above the earth in the expanse of the heavens.

21 And God created great sea monsters, and every living soul that moves with which the waters swarm, after their kind, and every winged fowl after its kind. And God saw that it was good.

22 And God blessed them, saying, Be fruitful and multiply, and fill the waters in the seas, and let fowl multiply on the earth.

23 And there was evening, and there was morning - a fifth day.

24 And God said, Let the earth bring forth living souls after their kind, cattle, and creeping thing, and beast of the earth, after their kind, And it was so.

25 And God made the beast of the earth after its kind, and the cattle after their kind, and every creeping thing of the ground after its kind. And God saw that it was good.

26 And God said, Let us make man in our image, after our likeness; and let them have dominion over the fish of the sea, and over the fowl of the heavens, and over the cattle, and over the whole earth, and over every creeping thing that creepeth on the earth.

27 And God created Man in his image, in the image of God created he him; male and female created he them.

28 And God blessed them; and said to them, Be fruitful and multiply, and fill the earth and subdue it; and have dominion over the fish of the sea, and over the fowl of the heavens, and over every other animal that moveth on the earth.

29 And God said, Behold I have given you every herb producing seed that is on the whole earth, and every tree in which is the fruit of a tree producing seed: it shall be food for you;

30 and to every animal of the earth, and to every fowl of the heavens, and to everything that creepeth on the earth, in which is a living soul, every green herb for food. And it was so.

31 And God saw everything that he had made, and behold it was very good. And there was evening, and there was morning – the sixth day." (Gen. 1:19-31 Darby Translation)

More verses showing that animals have living souls.

"And all flesh died that moved upon the earth, both of fowl, and of cattle, and of beast, and of every creeping thing that creepeth upon the earth, and every man, All in whose nostrils was the breath of life, of all that was in the dry land died." (Gen. 7:21-22 KJV) (Breath of life means a living soul – 'life' here means living soul – God's breath is what imparts a living soul)

"Who knoweth not in all these that the hand of the LORD hath wrought this? In whose hand is the soul of every living thing, and the breath of mankind." (Job 12:9-10 KJV)

"And levy a tribute unto the LORD of the men of war which went out to battle: one soul of five hundred, both of the persons and beeves. And of the asses, and of the sheep:" (Numbers 31:28 KJV)

And in Revelation we read:

"And the third part of the creatures which were in the sea, and had life, died; and the third part of the ships were destroyed." (Rev. 8:9 KJV) (Here 'life' means living soul.)

In Isaiah we read: "4 But with righteousness shall he judge the poor, and reprove with equity for the meek of the earth: and he shall smite the earth with the rod of his mouth, and with the breath of his lips shall he slay the wicked.

5 And righteousness shall be the girdle of his loins, and faithfulness the girdle of his reins.

6 The wolf shall also dwell with the lamb, and the leopard shall lie down with the kid; and the calf and the young lion and the fatling together; and a little child shall lead them.

7 And the cow and the bear shall feed; their young ones shall lie down together: and the lion shall eat straw like the ox.

8 And the suckling child shall play on the hole of the asp, and the weaned child shall put his hand on the cockatrice den.

9 They shall not hurt nor destroy in all my holy mountain: for the earth shall be full of the knowledge of the LORD, as the waters cover the sea." (Is. 11:4-9 KJV)

This is also spoken of in Isaiah 65.

Romans says, "19 For the earnest expectation of the creature (all creation) waiteth for the manifestation of the sons of God. (us true believers)

20 For the creature was made subject to vanity, not willingly, but by reason of him who hath subjected the same in hope,

21 Because the creature itself shall also be delivered from the bondage of corruption into the glorious liberty of the children of God.

22 For we know that the whole creation groaneth and travaileth in pain together until now." (Rom. 8:19-22 KJV)

At this point I just wanted to give you some evidence that all animals will have eternal life with the LORD. There is much, much more I could share but I will leave it here with this final thought.

All animals are innocent and have not sinned. Their spiritual connection with the LORD has never been broken as it has with man. The Garden of Eden is a picture of heaven and of the eternal connection with God. After Adam and Eve sin, man is driven out of the Garden – but animals are not. (see Gen. 3:24) this is indicating the spiritual bond between God and man was severed, but the spiritual bond between God and animals wasn't.

Animals of course suffer along with man because God put them under man's dominion. When the first Adam fell, animals automatically fell even though are innocent and still spiritually connected to God. They fell unwillingly – automatically.

Likewise, when the second Adam which is Christ died on the cross for our sins and was resurrected He automatically redeemed all the animals – they became saved and received eternal life automatically.

Because man chose to sin – He must choose salvation through Christ. Animals have no choice in either – they fell without choice and are saved without choice – automatic in both situations.

Those who have lost pets or other animals they love – take comfort, be joyful and be glad for the good news. The work of Christ is all encompassing, total and without lack, bringing about the redemption of all creation. All animals have eternal life and go to heaven – anything less would be incomplete. So, rejoice in the LORD – for He is good!

In my upcoming book I go much deeper.

MAN AND DOMINION

What is dominion?

Dominion means to rule over. It is a position of authority, of stewardship.

What about our role as stewards of God's creatures?

How should we as Christians treat His lesser creatures?

He has entrusted us with caring for His animals. We have a duty and an obligation to God to treat them well. And this goes deeper than duty and obligation. God loved us before we loved Him, but love of God is why we desire to serve Him according to His will. Ultimately if we are truly saved we will want to do His will out of our love for Him. This is beyond duty and obligation – it is a great honor and privilege to follow Him – to do His will. This desire comes from relationship – from being born again. And those who can't understand this or ignore this do so because they are not truly saved.

To harm animals without just cause or to ignore their suffering is to deny the love of God, to deny His will, and to dishonor and disrespect Him. It is to deny His position of Father and ours as sons and daughters. Beyond that, it is to deny our basic duty and obligation of stewardship – it is bad stewardship at the very least.

Those who can't understand or see this are spiritually blind. They can't see it or understand it because they are not truly born again – they are deceived not saved.

Death is the enemy. Pain and suffering are not part of God's Kingdom.

Biblically the only reasons to harm or kill an animal are: Old Testament – sacrifice, food (after the flood), self defense and as a side effect of warfare.

In the New Testament it is the same except that sacrifice has been removed because Jesus Christ was the ultimate sacrifice. So, today the only Biblical reasons to harm or kill an animal are for food, self defense or as a side effect of war.

There is no true man of God anywhere in the Bible who harms or kills animals without just cause. (As listed above) Why?

Because harming or killing animals without just cause is ungodly. No true man of God would do such a thing.

There are some in the Bible who unnecessarily hurt and kill animals – they are types of the anti-Christ, they are called wicked and evildoers, and are those opposed to God.

This is not meant to criticize or condemn, but rather to warn. There are a lot of people today who are deceived – there are a lot of false teachers who are leading people astray. And the consequences can be eternal. Today, we have pop cult figures, celebrities, politicians and even pastors and preachers who are leading many astray.

Jesus warns us not to be deceived – not all who call Him LORD will enter the Kingdom of Heaven.

I do not wish for anyone to make an eternal mistake. My hope is that this will help prevent that.

I do not believe anyone who harms or kills animals for any reasons other than those listed above are truly saved. This is not to say they are unsaved because of their actions.

But rather, their actions are evidence they are not really saved – they are deceived. As Jesus says, 'You will know them by their fruit'.

Today many people are doing bad things to animals for all kinds of reasons – none of them acceptable according to the word of God. (And the church is silent).

The list includes hunting for sport, animal testing research, factory farms mistreating farm animals, using animals in the production of pharmaceuticals and health supplements, poor breeding facilities, mistreating pets, killing animals in control centers, wildlife management programs that roundup and kill animals, sporting events which harm and kill, such as bear baying, horse tripping and bull fighting and more.

All of these activities are against the will of God, they are Biblically unsupported, and evidence of a heart that is not right with God.

If one is truly filled with the spirit of Christ then they will be changed and they will like what God likes and hate what God hates. They will hate all pain, all suffering and all death.

As Jesus said in His very first words in the New Testament – We must fulfill all righteousness. We must do everything that is right. This is about more than baptism; it is a prime directive from the LORD.

Those who are apathetic, tolerant of such things; or worse those who enjoy causing pain, suffering, and death without just cause are doing the work of Satan – not Christ.

Satan is the one who came to steal, kill and destroy. To derive pleasure from doing such things shows who such a person belongs to.

Harming, and killing animals without cause is the exact opposite of God's will – it is prideful and selfish –it is evidence of a hardened heart, a dark heart – it is evidence of a lack of Christ.

Doing such things is not simply back sliding or messing up or falling into temptation.

There is no temptation – it is not like an addiction – it is self will plain and simple. It is self will instead of God's will. This is always the real issue.

Satan and the fallen angels fell because of pride and self will – Adam and Eve did their own will as opposed to God's will. Cain did his own will as opposed to God's will.

It is always God's will vs. self will.

Make no mistake - self will is what the enemy uses to deceive you and trick you into believing a lie. The lie is that someone thinks they are saved when they are not.

When someone harms or kills an animal for any unjust reason they are doing self will – it is evidence of who they are spiritually connected to.

Many times animals are harmed or killed there is no reason at all – it simply because that is what someone wants to do.

When God gave us dominion He did not give us ownership. All animals belong to Him. Our position of dominion is one of caretaker – He gave us the awesome responsibility of taking care of His creatures. He placed us in this position of authority, which we are supposed to use correctly in accordance with His will.

How can someone claim to love the Father in heaven whom they can't see, yet harm, destroy and kill His creatures here on earth which they can see?

How can someone claim to love and respect God, yet harm and destroy His creation?

It is a great contradiction – it is double minded – it is not a whole hearted love of God.

We have a clear direct duty and obligation to God to care for His animals.

If you owned a retail store and hired me as manager, you would be placing me in a position of authority – a position of dominion and stewardship.

You would expect me to use my authority in accordance with your will – to open and close on time, make deposits on time, ring up sales properly, keep the place clean etc.

But, because of my position I would have the ability to do otherwise. I could open late and close early, break things, give merchandise to my friends, steal money and merchandise etc.

This would be an abuse of my position – it would be misusing my authority – it would be bad stewardship – it would be against your will – and you would probably fire me – and rightly so.

This is the same as God giving us dominion - placing us in a position of authority over His animals. He gave us stewardship over His creatures and we are supposed to use our position in accordance with His will.

Mistreating, hurting and killing His creatures without just cause is misusing and abusing our position of authority and dominion.

Jesus says not all who call Him LORD will enter heaven. He rejects those who do works of inequity – meaning those who are doing things which are unauthorized.

He also says the decisive issue is whether or not they are doing the Father's will.

A person's actions and works are the evidence of whether or not they are truly saved.

The invisible is known by the visible – we know who a person is serving by their fruit.

Do not be deceived.

In the parable of the wheat and tares, Jesus tells us the tares are planted among the wheat by the enemy – while the people slept. The church is asleep – and so there are tares in the church – do not let them lead you astray.

If you or someone you care about engages in hurting or killing animals unjustly – then it is time to repent. God can and will forgive, but this is a situation that requires repentance, because it is willful disobedience without temptation.

Also, consider the principle of sowing and reaping. God says that seed time and harvest time will always remain. This refers to the seasons and to sowing and reaping.

We reap what we sow – good or bad. If a person sows pain and suffering that is what they will eventually reap. This principle often reaches into households. David's son died because of what David did to Uriah.

When someone sows the seeds of pain and suffering and death, the reaping may take place in their household meaning their spouses, children or grandchildren as well as themselves.

Keep an eye out for this and you will see it manifest frequently. I notice that many people who harm and kill animals in any manner that is not Biblical bring physical pain and suffering into their houses. I see children born with terrible diseases, people having serious medical conditions, cancers, degenerative diseases etc. The list goes on – I see it over and over in plain sight. And this affects the household not just the individual. Be aware – look for this and you will start to notice it happens all the time.

It is sowing and reaping, plain and simple – they are reaping what they have sown. It never fails – in fact it never can fail – it has to happen, because it is a universal, eternal principle of God. For it not to happen would make His word untrue.

Keep in mind we are not talking about a true believer who messes up or falls into temptation or who makes a mistake. That is covered by mercy and grace.

But this different, because it is self will – no temptation – it is not a saved person messing up – it is a deceived, unsaved person intentionally rebelling against God.

It is not the act that makes the person unsaved – their action shows they are unsaved. They are not unsaved because of what they do – they do what they do because they are unsaved.

If they truly had the Spirit of Christ in them – Christ who is love, who is kind, merciful, just and righteous –they would find, pain, suffering and death to be intolerable, they would hate it in all its forms.

So, the fact that they are apathetic or tolerant of it; or actually enjoy causing pain and harm shows they do not truly have the Spirit of Christ in them.

What is it but the arrogance and vanity of man to use his position of authority and power to neglect, and abuse and harm those under him without cause?

It is wicked and evil.

The time is late – it is time to get real – to truly follow Christ – repent and follow Him. Set your mind on God's will and not your own before it is too late.

I will put some verses of scripture here – I pray that you will read them and see and hear and understand. Read them in the context of what has been shared.

Please don't misunderstand – this is not meant to criticize or condemn – but to warn - there are many who believe they are going to be with the LORD forever who are not – because they lack understanding – like the Pharisees – because they lack understanding they have religion, but they can't understand what the Spirit is saying and are not saved.

I pray you understand and hear what the Spirit is saying. Do not let yourself be deceived. Seek the truth – the true word of God – now is the time to put aside all falseness and pursue Him in all righteousness.

Let me mention one more thing before I present scripture.

As Christians we are supposed to be representatives or ambassadors of Christ. This is why Paul tells us to avoid all appearance of doing evil.

Non Christians (potential Christians) are going to watch and they will make a decision about Christ and Christianity based on how they see (so-called) Christians act.

They will likely choose to accept or reject Christ based on what they see "Christians" do.

If someone has a heart for God's creatures and loves animals, and then sees someone claiming to be a Christian who engages in harming them or killing them for no just reason – what will that person think?

That person who loves animals will think of the so-called Christian as a hypocrite and phony – and will very likely reject Christ and Christianity because of the false impression.

The question is this. Are your actions leading people to Christ or turning them away? Are people rejecting Christ and Christianity because they see so-called Christians doing ungodly things all the while claiming to be Christians? How many are turned away because of this?

The Bible says not to give any ground to the enemy. There are a lot of people who love animals who reject Christ and Christianity because of these things. The Devil loves this.

We can't give up ground like this.

We are supposed to be the light – we are supposed to let our good works shine brightly before men in order to help draw them to Christ.

What type of influence might some of those people have? Some of those who have rejected Christ and Christianity could be leaders, they could be people capable of great influence, they could be politicians, perhaps even a congressperson or president – or maybe just a celebrity with influence or a media person with influence. How much influence for Christ and Christianity is being lost due to this?

Imagine if most of the people who love animals and fight for animal rights were to accept Jesus Christ as LORD – imagine the difference that could make in our nation – imagine how many souls could be won for Christ.

Imagine if all Christians spoke up, fought for, and cared for God's creation and His lesser creatures. Imagine.

This is my mission.

"Many pastors have destroyed my vineyard, they have trodden my portion under foot, they have made my pleasant portion a desolate wilderness. They have made it desolate, and being desolate it mourneth unto me; the whole land is made desolate, because no man layeth it to heart.

The spoilers are come upon all high places through the wilderness: for the sword of the LORD shall devour from the one end of the land even unto the other end of the land: no flesh shall have peace." (Jeremiah 12:10-12 KJV)

Disrespecting His creation and His creatures is disrespecting Him.

God will devour and destroy those who do so – and a nation that does so will be devoured from one end to the other – and will not have peace.

Let's go to the word of God.

"Let the heaven and earth praise him, the seas, and everything that moveth therein." (Ps 69:34 KJV)

"10 You make the springs pour water into ravines, so streams gush down from the mountains.

11 They provide water for all the animals, and the wild donkeys quench their thirst.

12 The birds nest beside the streams and sing among the branches of the trees.

13 You send rain on the mountains from your heavenly home, and you fill the earth with the fruit of your labor.

14 You cause the grass to grow for the cattle. You cause plants to grow for people to use. You allow them to produce food from the earth –

15 wine to make them glad, olive oil as lotion for their skin, and bread to give them strength.

16 The trees of the LORD are well cared for – the cedars of Lebanon that he planted.

17 There the birds make their nests, and the storks make their homes in the firs.

18 High in the mountains are pastures for the wild goats, and the rocks form a refuge for rock badgers.

19 You made the moon to mark the seasons and the sun that knows when to set.

20 You send the darkness, and it becomes night, when all the forest animals prowl about.

21 Then the young lions roar for their food, but they are dependent on God.

22 At dawn they slink back into their dens to rest.

23 Then the people go off to their work; they labor until the evening shadows fall again.

24 O LORD, what a variety of things you have made! In wisdom you have made them all. The earth is full of your creatures.

25 Here is the ocean, vast and wide, teeming with life of every kind, both great and small.

26 See the ships sailing along, and Leviathan, which you made to play in the sea.

27 Every one of these depends on you to give them food as they need it.

28 When you supply it, they gather it. You open your hand to feed them, and they are satisfied.

29 But if you turn away from them, they panic. When you take away their breath, they die and turn again to dust.

30 When you send your Spirit, new life is born to replenish all the living of the earth.

31 May the glory of the LORD last forever! The LORD rejoices in all he has made!

32 The earth trembles at his glance; the mountains burst into flame at his touch.

33 I will sing to the LORD as long as I live. I will praise my God to my last breath!

34 May he be pleased by all these thoughts about him, for I rejoice in the LORD.

35 Let all sinners vanish from the face of the earth; let the wicked disappear forever. As for me – I will praise the LORD! Praise the LORD!"

(Ps. 104:10-35 Tyndale NLT)

"Simeon and Levi are two of a kind – men of violence.

O my soul, stay away from them. May I never be a party to their wicked plans.

For in their anger they murdered men,

And they crippled oxen just for sport.

Cursed be their anger, for it is fierce;

Cursed be their wrath, for it is cruel.

Therefore I will scatter their descendants throughout the nation of Israel." (Gen. 49:5-8 Tyndale NLT)

The bible says that harming animals for sport is wicked and cruel.

Simeon and Levi here are wicked for both murder and crippling oxen for sport – they are considered wicked for each of these things. They are in effect doubly wicked and cruel – hence we see them being cursed twice.

In the King James Version they are called 'instruments of cruelty'.

"Then the LORD caused the donkey to speak. 'What have I done to you that deserves you beating me these three times?' it asked Balaam.

'Because you have made me look like a fool!' Balaam shouted. If I had sword with me, I would kill you!'

'But I am the same donkey you always ride on', the donkey answered. 'Have I ever done anything like this before?'

'No', he admitted.

Then the LORD opened Balaam's eyes, and he saw the angel of the LORD standing in the roadway with a drawn sword in his hand. Balaam fell face down on the ground before him.

'Why did you beat your donkey those three times?' the angel of the LORD demanded.

(Numbers 22:28-32 Tyndale NLT)

Balaam was on his way at the request of Balak, who wanted Balaam to curse Israel.

So, the angel of the LORD is angry with Balaam for two reasons. One for listening to Balak and the other for hitting his donkey without cause.

Later, in the story, the angel of the LORD says, he was about to slay Balaam and save the donkey. And notice the language – the angel of the LORD demanded.

While there are many things going on here, we know the angel of the LORD was very angry that Balaam harmed his donkey without just cause. In fact he was ready to kill him right there.

I believe 'the angel of the LORD', is Jesus Christ himself. The angel of the LORD is Christ pre-incarnate.

This phrase implies there is only one like him.

Our position of Dominion is not ownership. God owns all the animals.

"10 For every beast of the forest is mine, and the cattle upon a thousand hills. I know all the fowls of the mountains: and the wild beasts of the field are mine." (Ps. 50:10-11 KJV)

The word 'know' here in the original Hebrew is yada. This word has many meanings, but generally it means to know with certainty, to know intimately.

"Thou art worthy, O Lord, to receive glory and honor, and power: for thou hast created all things, and for thy pleasure they are and were created" (Rev. 4:11 KJV)

And, it is God's will that they multiply and fill the earth.

If a person harms or kills an animal unnecessarily they are stealing from God, they are taking what belongs to Him, out their own self will for no just cause. They are denying God the pleasure He created them for.

We could say – they are denying God, period.

They are not caring about the will of God – just what pleases them.

Is such a person really saved?

No. The evidence says otherwise.

Such people are not unsaved because of what they do.

But rather, they do such things because they are unsaved.

If they were truly saved they would only hurt or kill when absolutely necessary.

What would Jesus do?

"The thief's purpose is to steal, kill and destroy. My purpose is to give life in all its fullness." (Jn. 10:10 Tyndale NLT)

"The nations were angry with you, but now the time of your wrath has come. It is time to judge the dead and reward your servants. You will reward your prophets, and your holy people, all who fear your name, from the least to the greatest. And you will destroy those who have caused destruction on the earth." (Rev.11:18 NLT)

Bad stewardship is a serious matter.

Hurting, injuring, killing and destroying are not part of God's Kingdom. Killing is destroying life, which God created. There will be a heavy price to pay for those who do such things unjustly, without cause.

According to the Bible, they will not enter the Kingdom of Heaven, but will be destroyed.

"1 Let every soul be subject to the higher powers. For there is no power but of God: the powers that be are ordained of God.

2 Whosoever therefore resisteth the power, resisteth the ordinance of God: and they that resist shall receive to themselves damnation.

3 For rulers are not a terror to good works, but to the evil. Wilt thou then not be afraid of the power? Do that which is good, and thou shalt have praise of the same:

4 For he is the minister of God to thee for good. But, if thou do that which is evil, be afraid; for he beareth not the sword in vain: for he is the minister of God, a revenger to execute wrath upon him that doeth evil." (Rom. 13:1-4 KJV)

We all want God's mercy, not His judgment. God has dominion over us. If we want mercy from the one who has dominion over us; then shouldn't we be merciful to those under our dominion?

Understand this section is not meant to be critical or to condemn. The purpose is to warn those who are in danger. I believe there are a lot of people who call themselves Christians who are in danger and need this warning.

They are in danger because although they know the scriptures, they don't understand. Understanding the meaning of the word is vital in these last days and vital to one's eternal destiny. Misunderstanding or not understanding can eternally separate you from the LORD.

People perish for a lack of understanding. The Hebrew word "knowledge" is da'at", which means "knowledge; understanding". It is essentially knowledge and understanding.

In the verse below the most accurate interpretation would be to use the phrase "knowledge and understanding" where we see "knowledge".

"My people are destroyed for a lack of knowledge: because thou hast rejected knowledge, I will also reject thee, that thou shall be no priest in me: seeing thou hast forgotten the law of thy God, I will also forget thy children" (Hos. 4:6 KJV)

Jesus mentions those who will perish many times.

Dominion is a position of authority and stewardship. We should use this position of dominion and authority correctly to care for God's animals and His creation in accordance with His will.

"And the Lord God took the man, and placed him into the Garden of Eden to dress it and to keep it." (Gen. 2:15 KJV)

Or we can disobey God and abuse our position of dominion and authority to do harm, injure, neglect and kill His animals without just cause.

Death is the enemy.

Pain, suffering and death all came about as the result of the fall – these things are all satanic in nature.

It is time to wake up.

"1 And to the angel of the church in Sardis write; These things saith he that hath the seven Spirits of God, and the seven stars; I know thy works, that thou hast a name that thou livest, and art dead.

2 Be watchful, and strengthen the things which remain, that are ready to die: for I have not found thy works perfect before God.

3 Remember therefore how thou hast received and heard, and hold fast, and repent. If therefore thou shalt not watch, I will come on thee as a thief, and thou shalt not know what hour I will come upon thee.

4 Thou hast a few names even in Sardis which have not defiled their garments; and they shall walk with me in white: for they are worthy.

5 He that overcometh, the same shall be clothed in white raiment; and I will not blot out his name out of the book of life, but I will confess his name before my Father, and before his angels.

6 He that hath an ear, let him hear what the Spirit saith unto the churches." (Rev. 3: 1-6 KJV)

Don't be deceived. Not all who say Jesus Christ is LORD are truly saved. Do not let false teachers lead you astray.

"Enter ye at the straight gate: for wide is the gate, and broad is the way, that leadeth to destruction, and many there be which go in there at: Because straight is the gate, and narrow is the way, which leadeth unto life, and few there be that find it.

Beware of false prophets, which come to you in sheep's clothing, but inwardly they are ravenous wolves.

Ye shall know them by their fruits. Do men gather grapes of thorns, or figs of thistles? Even so every good tree bringeth forth good fruit; but a corrupt tree bringeth forth evil fruit.

A good tree cannot bring forth evil fruit, neither can a corrupt tree bring forth good fruit. Every tree that bringeth not forth good fruit is hewn down and cast into the fire.

Wherefore by their fruits you shall know them.

Not everyone that saith unto me, Lord, Lord, shall enter into the Kingdom of Heaven; but he that doeth the will of my Father which is in heaven." (Matt. 7:13-21 KJV)

Harming animals without cause is against the will of our Father, which was demonstrated in the Garden of Eden.

"Not all people who sound religious are really godly. They may refer to me as 'Lord', but they still won't enter the Kingdom of Heaven. The decisive issue is whether they obey my Father in heaven. On judgment day many will tell me, 'Lord, Lord, we prophesied in your name and cast out demons in your name and performed many miracles in your name.' But I will reply, 'I never knew you. Go away; the things you did were unauthorized.'" (Matt.7:21-23 Tyndale NLT)

"I Beseech you therefore, brethren, by the mercies of God, that ye present your bodies a living sacrifice, holy, acceptable unto God, which is your reasonable service.

And be not conformed to this world: but be ye transformed by the renewing of your mind, that ye may prove what is that good, and acceptable, and perfect, will of God" (Rom. 12:1-2 KJV)

Dominion goes to authority – harming and killing animals without cause is an abuse of authority – it is against the will of God – we are able to because of our position, but it is unauthorized – God never gave us the authority to harm and kill any creature without cause.

"For whosoever shall do the will of my Father which is in heaven, the same is my brother, and sister, and mother." (Matt. 12:50 KJV)

Those who do their own self will and not God's will are self deceived.

They do their own will because they are deceived – and not born again.

They are spiritually dead.

"Then shall the Kingdom of Heaven be likened unto ten virgins, which took their lamps, and went forth to meet the bridegroom.

And five of them were wise, and five were foolish.

They that were foolish took their lamps, and took no oil with them: But the wise took oil in their vessels with their lamps.

While the bridegroom tarried, they all slumbered and slept. And at midnight there was a cry made, Behold, the bridegroom cometh; go ye out to meet him.

Then all those virgins arose, and trimmed their lamps.

And the foolish said unto the wise, Give us of your oil; for our lamps have gone out.

But the wise answered, saying, Not so; lest there not be enough for us and you: but go ye rather to them that sell, and buy for yourselves.

And while they went to buy, the bridegroom came; and they that were ready went in with him to the marriage: and the door was shut.

Afterward came also the other virgins, saying, Lord, Lord, open to us.

But, he answered and said, Verily I say unto you, I know you not.

Watch therefore, for ye know neither the day nor the hour wherin the Son of man cometh." (Matt. 25:1-13 KJV)

Why five out of ten? Why not seven or eight or three? Because, it will be five out of ten – 50%.

In these verses keep in mind Jesus Christ is speaking to His disciples, not outsiders, not the public at large. He is talking to his followers.

The ten virgins represent those who are expecting to go to be with the Lord Jesus Christ. The oil represents the Spirit of Christ in them – the Holy Spirit. Five have it, five do not. Five are spiritually alive in Christ and five are spiritually dead. (50%)

In the parable of the prodigal son it is the older one - the one who has been in the house – in church – a long time who ultimately does not go into the feast – because of his own self will. (50%)

It is the same root problem we see in the story of Cain and Abel. (50%) This is not a sin offering so no blood is required – it is a harvest offering so it is ok for Cain to bring produce.

(Note: this is after God has clothed Adam and Eve with animal skins - a fore-shadow of Passover and of Christ's death – the next main feast on the calendar is the fall harvest - next in the Bible we see the tale of Cain and Abel. BTW: the literal English meaning of the opening words in this story are: "At the end of days' Cain brought ...")

Abel brought his best to the LORD because he trusted God and was focused on God and not himself – he was following the spirit – being God centered not self centered. Cain on the other hand brought his leftovers because he didn't really believe God. He was following his nature – he was self centered and self focused. Like the older son, he had religion not relationship, he was just going through the motions. He was self centered, self focused. He did his will - not God's.

Self will is fatal – it is the evidence of someone who does not really believe God or God's word. It is the evidence of one who is all about self, not God. It is the evidence of one who is not saved.

Don't be deceived.

Actions are the evidence of who we belong to. By their fruit you will know them.

"Woe unto the world because of offences! for it must needs be that offences come; but woe unto that man by whom the offence cometh!" (Matt. 18:7 KJV)

"1 Praise the LORD!

> Praise the LORD from the heavens!

> > Praise him from the skies!

2 Praise him, all his angels!

> Praise him, all the armies of heaven!

3 Praise him, sun and moon!

> Praise him, all you twinkling stars.

4 Praise him, skies above!

> Praise him, vapors high above the clouds!

5 Let every created thing give praise to the LORD, for he issued his command, and they came into being.

6 He established them forever and forever, His orders will never be revoked.

7 Praise the LORD from the earth, you creatures of the ocean depths,

8 fire, hail, snow and storm, wind and weather that obey him,

9 mountains and hills, fruit trees and all cedars,

10 wild animals and all livestock, reptiles and birds,

11 kings of the earth and all people, rulers and judges of the earth,

12 young men and maidens, old men and children.

13 Let them all praise the name of the LORD, For his name is very great; his glory towers over the earth and heaven!

14 He has made his people strong, honoring his godly ones – the people of Israel who are close to him.

Praise the LORD!" (Ps. 148, Tyndale NLT)

The time is now to truly be who God called us to be.

It is time to put aside falseness.

It is time to follow Jesus Christ our LORD and Savior.

It is time to be real. It is time to wake up.

Repent before it is too late.

Come to Christ in all honesty, truthfully for His glory.

It is the time to put God first.

It is time to do His will.

Let our works show the goodness and glory of the LORD.

In closing,

My favorite psalm:

"1 The LORD is my shepherd; I shall not want.

2 He maketh me to lie down in green pastures: he leadeth me besides the still waters.

3 He restoreth my soul: he leadeth me in the paths of righteousness for his name's sake.

4 Yea, though I walk through the valley of the shadow of death, I will fear no evil: for thou art with me; thy rod and thy staff they comfort me.

5 Thou preparest a table before me in the presence of mine enemies: thou anointest my head with oil; my cup runneth over.

6 Surely goodness and mercy shall follow me all the days of my life: and I will dwell in the house of the LORD forever." (Psalm 23 KJV)

May God Bless You,

And Peace be with you in the name of Jesus Christ,

Henry A. Rhyne

P.S. Please review this book on Amazon.com.

Please visit *www.KoahWisdom.com* and my youtube channel KoahWisdom and tell others. It is a new channel but I am posting a lot of great teaching videos there.

Also, please consider helping out. If you would like help me continue my mission and work you can give a gift at the above website or by sending a check to:

Henry A. Rhyne 201C Alston Blvd. #45, Hampstead, NC. 28443

I have not formed a nonprofit yet so this **is not tax deductible,** but the IRS does allow gifts up to $14,000 per year without any reporting requirements – any amount would be greatly appreciated.

If you just want to communicate you can send a note or letter to the above address – I will do my best to get back to you soon.

Also, please consider helping animals by giving to an animal welfare organization. They need us to help and to speak up for them. You can be a doer of the word by helping out.

Here is a list of some good organizations with their contact information.

General Animal Welfare

ASPCA (aspca.org) 424 East 92nd Street, New York, NY. 10128

The Humane Society of The United States (humanesociety.org) 2100 L Street NW, Washington D.C. 20037

Doris Day Animal League (ddal.org) 2100 L Street, NW Washington D.C. 20037

Humane Society Legislative Fund (hslf.org) 2100 L Street NW, suite 310, Washington D.C. 20037

Organizations that specialize in helping farm animals:

Farm Sanctuary (farmsanctuary.org) P.O. Box 150 Watkins Glen, New York, 14891-0150

Animals' Angels (animalsangels.org) P.O. Box 5003 Hagerstown, MD. 21741-5003 (They also help domestic animals - dogs& cats etc.)

Organizations that specialize in helping wildlife:

Sierra Club (SierraClub.org) 85 Second Street, San Francisco, CA. 94105-3456

Defenders of Wildlife (defenders.org) 1130 17th Street NW, Washington, DC 20036

Organizations that specialize in helping horses: Horses are a noble part of our nation's heritage, and because of our government's policies they are nearing extinction in the wild and are suffering many horrific things.

Wild Horse Freedom Federation, Inc. (wildhorsefreedomfederation.org) P.O. Box 390, Pinehurst, TX. 77354

Equine Voices Rescue & Sanctuary (equinevoices.org) P.O. Box 9597 Pueblo, CO. 81008-6077

LifeSavers Wild Horse Rescue (wildhorserescue.org) P.O. Box 939, Bakersfield, CA. 93302-0939

All of these organizations are doing fine work helping God's creatures. There are many fine organizations and so many animals that need our help (we are their stewards). Obviously we can't do it all or give to all. There is only so much we can do. But we should do what we can. Every little bit helps and if we all do a little, together we can accomplish a great deal. So, please consider doing something. We can make a real difference – for the glory of God – all good works should be celebrated for the glory of the Lord - to shine a light in a dark world – to draw all people closer to God.

Thank You,

And again, May God Bless You.

Henry A. Rhyne

Made in the USA
Middletown, DE
14 December 2015